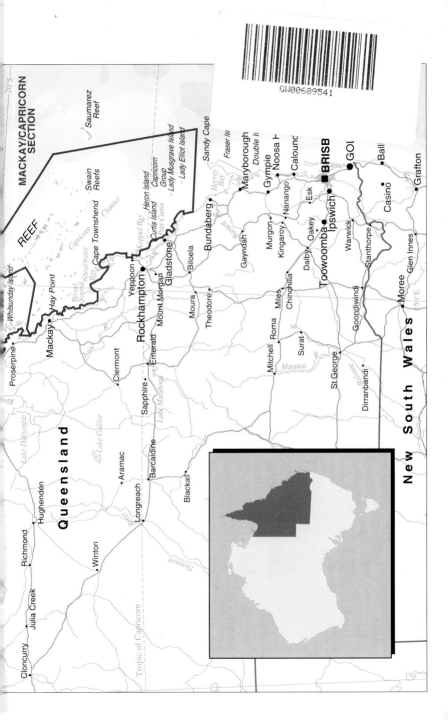

Australia's Great Barrier Reef

Little Hills Press

© Little Hills Press, 1996
Photographs by Far North Queensland Promotion Bureau, Tourism Mackay,
Townsville Enterprise Ltd, Eduard Domin, Great Barrier Reef Marine Park
Authority. **We gratefully acknowledge the assistance of these bodies in
helping to make this book a reality.**
Cover by IIC
Maps drawn by 🌐 **MAPgraphics**

This edition March 1996
ISBN 1 86315 060 9

Produced by Fay Smith and LHP editorial staff.

Little Hills Press
Regent House
37-43 Alexander Street
Crows Nest NSW 2065
Australia

Moorland Publishing Company
Moor Farm Road
Airfield Estate, Ashbourne
Derbyshire DE6 1HD
England
ISBN 0 86190 337 4

Inside Back Cover: Tubastrea sp.
Facing Title Page: Coral
Facing page 16: Clown Fish

LITTLE HILLS PRESS is a member
of **PUBLISH** *Australia*

DISCLAIMER
Whilst all care has been taken by the publisher and authors to ensure
that the information is accurate and up to date, the publisher does not
take responsibility for the information published herein. The
recommendations are those of the author, and as things get better or
worse, places close and others open, some elements in the book may be
inaccurate when you get there. Please write and tell us about it so we
can update in subsequent editions.

Front Cover: Scuba Diving off one of the islands in the Great Barrier
Reef. **Back Cover:** A typical beach scene in the Townsville Area.

CONTENTS

AUSTRALIA'S
GREAT BARRIER REEF

The Great Barrier Reef extends 2030km from Breaksea Spit on the Queensland coast of Australia (south of the Tropic of Capricorn), to the coastal waters of New Guinea, making it the longest series of coral reefs and islands in the world. It consists of thousands of atolls, islands, shoals, reefs and coral formations that combine to form a barrier between the Pacific Ocean swells and the calmer coastal waters.

Scientists estimate that the Reef has grown from the seabed, involving billions of coral polyps over a period of around 500,000 years, and the living coral is still on the job today. The Reef has attracted a plethora of living things so interactive with each other that they and the Reef have become one living organism.

When the Matthew Flinders expedition circumnavigated Australia in 1802, many previously unknown parts of its coastline were charted. In 1815 Charles Jeffreys sailed the entire length of the Queensland coast, inside the Reef, and in 1819 Phillip King completed the task of charting the Reef. His report established that taking the route inside the reef was the quickest and safest way to sail along Australia's north-eastern coast.

CHARACTERISTICS

From the northern end, the Reef lies close to the coastline for about a thousand kilometres; towards the southern end it veers away and breaks into a series of wide reefs that have proven to be shipping hazards in the past because of deceptively deep water between the shoals. In some places the outer edges of the reefs are less than 16km from the shore; in others they are as much as 320km.

The southern waters of the Reef are home to the reefs and

bays of the *Bunker* and *Capricorn* groups, considered by some to be the most beautiful of the Reef's coral formations. Elsewhere, the coral and reef life are not in such profusion.

Heron Island, with an area of 17ha, lies on the Tropic of Capricorn, and is home to a Marine Biological Research Station. Heron, in common with the larger islands of the Reef, is a National Park, which is good news for the green turtles who come to lay their eggs each November, and the mutton birds and terns who nest on the island.

Great Keppel Island, off Yeppoon, and *Quoin*, in Port Curtis, are close to the coast, high and rocky, and have resorts. Further north are the *Percy Islands* and groups of similar islands that are virtually untouched.

The *Whitsunday Passage* is north of Mackay, and was founded and named by Captain Cook on Whitsunday 1770. The passage divides the *Cumberland Islands* from others nearer to the coast, including the resort islands of *Long, Brampton, Lindeman, Hamilton, South Molle, Whitsunday, Daydream* and *Hayman*. All these islands can be reached by plane and helicopter services from Mackay or Proserpine, a further 130km north. A cruise through the Whitsundays is high on the list of 'most popular holidays' for Australians as well as overseas visitors.

From Bowen, north of Proserpine, to Cairns, there are clusters of rocky islands, cays and coral reefs along the coast. The most accessible island is *Magnetic*, 8km from Townsville, then further north are *Great Palm, Orpheus, Hinchinbrook, Bedarra* and *Dunk*. With the exception of Great Palm Island, each has at least one resort and also other accommodation available.

Off-shore from Cairns are *Fitzroy* and *Green Islands*, with accommodation available on Green Island, as well as an underwater observatory, and a reef aquarium.

HISTORY

Australia's aboriginal people not only knew of the existence of the Reef, they had large outrigger canoes that enabled them to travel to the islands and outer reefs. They moved their settlements up and down the coast for thousands of years before the coming of the Europeans.

Sixteenth century maps include parts of the north and east coasts of Australia, but do not contain warnings of any hazards to shipping. It is known that Spanish, Chinese and Portuguese sailors were familiar with the Timor area and other parts to the north of Australia. For example, the 1606 expedition of Captain Torres in the caravel *San Pedrico* sailed through the strait that has been named in his honour. So it is possible that someone ventured further south, but there is no record of any one having done so.

Captain James Cook is the first person to record the existence of a reef as he sailed up the eastern coast of the continent. He first noticed shoals in the vicinity of Great Keppel Island, but he managed to continue north through the Whitsunday Passage, christening features and islands along the way. The *Endeavour* finally ran aground on a small reef near present day Cape Tribulation, and only expert seamanship enabled the ship to limp more than 70km to the mouth of a river where repairs could be carried out. Today the river is called the Endeavour, and the settlement on its banks is Cooktown.

Two months later when the *Endeavour* was as ship-shape as possible, Cook decided to try for the open sea, but could not find a way through the natural barrier. He sailed north, searching for a passage and reached Lizard Island, which he named because of its large population of those reptiles. Landing on the island, he and his botanist, Joseph Banks, climbed to its highest point and were able to see a break in the reef large enough to permit the passage of the *Endeavour*. On today's maps this is still known as Cook's Passage.

The first charts of the Reef were the work of another intrepid Englishman, Captain Matthew Flinders. He left Sydney on July 22, 1802, in the *Investigator*, and sailed up the north coast into the inner passage of the Reef. Using the technique of sending small boats ahead to sound the depths, Flinders charted a safe passage through the Reef, which is still known as Flinders' Passage. In fact, the soundings on his maps have been in use until quite recently. Incidentally, it was Flinders who gave the reef its name, Great Barrier Reef.

FLORA & FAUNA

When the Australian Government nominated the Great Barrier Reef for inclusion on the World Heritage List, it put forth the following:

The Great Barrier Reef is by far the largest single collection of coral reefs in the world. Biologically the Great Barrier Reef supports the most diverse ecosystem known to man. Its enormous diversity is thought to reflect the maturity of an ecosystem which has evolved over millions of years on the north-east continental shelf of Australia.

The Great Barrier Reef provides some of the most spectacular scenery on earth and is of exceptional natural beauty. The Great Barrier Reef provides major feeding ground for large populations of the endangered species *Dugong dugon* and contains nesting grounds of world significance for the endangered turtle species green turtle (*Chelonia mydas*) and loggerhead turtle (*Caretta caretta*).

The area nominated also meets the condition of integrity in that it includes the area of the sea adjacent to the Reef. The areas of this nomination contain many middens and other archaeological sites of Aboriginal or Torres Strait Islander origin. There are over 30 shipwrecks in the area, and on the islands, many of which are Queensland National Parks, there are ruins and operating lighthouses which are of cultural and historical significance.

The Great Barrier Reef was inscribed on the World Heritage List on October 26, 1981.

Fauna

Dugongs are herbivorous marine mammals, who look a bit like fat dolphins but are actually related to the elephant. The early explorers, who must have all needed glasses, mistook the creatures for mermaids, in spite of their particularly unattractive snout.

As well as the turtles mentioned in the above nomination, the hawksbill turtle is found on the Reef. It is the scale of this turtle that is sold, in other countries I hasten to add, as "tortoise shell". Turtles are protected by law, and only

Aborigines and Torres Strait Islanders are allowed to catch them as part of their cultural heritage. They are not permitted to sell any of their catch.

There are literally thousands of species of fish found living on the Reef, from small blennies who live on the bottom, to giant manta rays that can grow to seven metres across. In between there are fish of every size, shape and colour.

Other marine animals who make the waters of the Reef their home include sponges, worms, prawns, crabs, sea shells, sea-stars and sea squirts. Then, of course, there are the various coral polyps, which create living coral colonies. These are found in a variety of shapes and sizes that depend on how the individual polyps build their frames and bud off new polyps. Dead corals make up a reef, bound together by their own limestone and that of plant skeletons. Over thousands of years this reef of dead coral grows to many metres thick, always covered with a coating of living corals. Coral spawning takes place in November/December each year, beginning a night or two after the full moon and lasting for about six nights. This event is unknown in any other part of the animal kingdom.

That brings us to the infamous Crown of Thorns Starfish (*Acanthaster planci*), which is a predator that eats the coral polyps. Scientists have differing theories about this animal, which incidentally occurs in other areas of the Pacific, but they are keeping a close watch on their habitats and numbers.

Not permanent residents of the Reef, but annual visitors, are the Humpback Whales. From July to October they can be found throughout much of the warm, shallow waters. Their smaller cousins, dolphins and porpoises, are also regular visitors.

Land Animals

For obvious reasons the islands are not overrun with land species, but some have colonies of flying foxes, or fruit bats, and others have a few wallabies, and possibly some bandicoots. Magnetic Island is also home to koalas and possums.

Birds

Many of the islands of the Reef are home to seabirds and wading birds, as well as over 150 other species. Seagulls, cormorants, pelicans and terns are some of the common species, but less common include shearwaters, petrels, boobies, tropicbirds and frigatebirds. The Great Barrier Reef Marine Park Authority produce a series of Reef Notes, and the one entitled *Seabirds* gives more information on the different species, and also advises how bird colonies should be approached to lessen the human impact.

Flora

There are sixty-five vegetated sand cays in the Barrier Reef region. Some of them have only one or two species of salt tolerant plants, others have up to forty species, including rainforest trees.

Some of the islands have mangrove forests, and some have varied plant life, it all depends on the richness of the soil, and the rainfall.

PROTECTING THE ENVIRONMENT

The Great Barrier Reef Marine Park is divided into sections, each of which has several zones.

General Use 'A' Zone - line fishing and spear fishing, bait netting and gathering, crabbing and oyster gathering, diving, boating, trawling, and all reasonable uses are permitted.

General Use 'B' Zone - reasonable uses are permitted, but no trawling.

Marine National Park 'A' Zone - recreational use is permitted, ie fishing with one line and one hook is OK but no netting; diving is fine.

Marine National Park 'B' Zone - fishing is not permitted, but diving and photography are allowed.

Scientific Research Zone - off-bounds for all except the scientific fraternity.

Preservation Zone - completely off-limits except in cases of emergency.

Maps showing the various zones are readily available, and care should be taken to ensure that you do not enter a prohibited area.

Following is a list of things that visitors can do to play their part in protecting the environment.

The Reef
- Do not "souvenir" any animal or plant, whether dead or alive. This includes shells and corals.
- Always replace anything that you have moved.
- If in charge of a boat, always anchor with care. Use moorings when provided, or try to anchor in sand making sure that the chain and rope will not foul coral.

Camping
- Use fireplaces where provided, not an open fire. Make sure the fire is out when you leave the campsite. Do not collect firewood from the reserve.
- It is preferable to use a fuel stove for cooking.
- Enquire about the availability of water at your chosen destination. It may be that you have to take drinking water with you.
- Use bins where provided, or take all rubbish when you leave.
- If toilets are not provided at camp sites, bury human wastes.
- Do not take domestic animals into National Parks and Forests.
- Do not use soap in freshwater lakes and streams.

Animals
- Do not disturb nesting seabirds.
- Keep to designated walking tracks through the forests.
- Do not feed silver gulls - their increased numbers are a threat to other birds.
- In summer, when the female turtle is crawling up the beach and digging her nest, make sure the beach is dark and quiet. She is easily disturbed and will return to the

sea if frightened. Once she begins to lay her eggs she can be observed closely, and low lights can be used until she begins to return to the sea.

When the baby turtles are hatching, the use of lights confuses them and they will head for the light instead of the sea, with disastrous results.

CLIMATE

Situated off the coast in the State of Queensland, the entire Great Barrier Reef is in the tropics, so it is never cold, just varies between very warm and very hot.

Rockhampton, near the southernmost point of the Reef has January average temperatures of 31C (88F) max, 22C (72F) min. The July averages are 23C (73F) max, 9C (48F) min.

Cairns in the far north of Queensland has average January temperatures of 32C (90F) max, 24C (75F) min, and July temperatures of 25C (77F) max, 16C (61F) min.

In summer (December-February) the humidity is high, and if there is any chance of a cyclone, which can happen every few years, this is the season for it. Even if that doesn't eventuate, late summer is the wettest time of the year.

Consequently, the best time to visit the area is from May to October.

POPULATION

The populated areas on the eastern coast of Queensland range from cities like Cairns, with around 70,000 residents, to small fishing villages with a couple of hundred people. The closest State Capital is Brisbane with around 1.2 million inhabitants.

LANGUAGE

Australians speak English - with a few variations. Some of these we have borrowed from the English themselves, some from the Americans, and others we have sort of "made up" ourselves. Many of Australia's newest residents still have traces of their mother tongues, so add to the above Italian Australian, Greek Australian, Chinese Australian, and so on.

Visitors from overseas comment that we have a distinctive accent, but you can ask any Australian and they will tell you that we don't have an accent at all - everybody else does.

Australians **do** tend to speak very quickly, though, but mostly we are friendly souls who do not mind repeating what we've said, or changing it completely into a set of different words with the same meaning.

Unlike people from different parts of the United Kingdom and the United States, there is hardly any difference between the speech of someone who lives in Tasmania and someone from Darwin, at least not enough for a visitor to notice.

RELIGION

Australia has complete freedom of religion, and churches and temples from all faiths are found in all cities and some towns.

FESTIVALS

Christmas Day, New Year's Day, Easter and Anzac Day (April 25) are the only holidays that are held at the same time throughout the country. Queensland also has:

January 26 - Australia Day
May - (first Monday) - Labour Day
June - (second Monday) - Queen's Birthday.

Queensland's tropical north also has the following annual events:

January - Geogetown Turf Club Race
- Fitzroy 2000 Yacht Race
February - Opening of Barramundi Season
Lindeman Island Yacht Race
Hamilton Island Yacht Race
Langford Reef Yacht Race
March - Sunday Picnic Races - Cairns
World Barramundi Fishing Championships -Burketown
Sea Week Festival - Mackay
Sunflower Festival - Emerald
Cid Harbour Yacht Race

April	- Bushman's Rodeo - Cairns
	Hamilton Island Race Week
	Anzac Day Races - Mareeba
	Mackay Maltese Festival
	Golden Mount Festival - Mt Morgan
	Whitsunday Easter Games
	The Great Whitsunday Boating Regatta
May	- May Day Yachting Regatta - Whitsundays
	Tropical Garden Expo - Cairns
	Thursday Island Cultural Festival
June	- XXXX 2000 Regatta
	FNQ District Golf Championship - Cairns
	The Valley Heritage Festival - Mackay
	Hamilton Cup Outrigger Regatta
	Proserpine Show
July	- Atherton Show
	Mossman Agricultural Show
	Australian Festival of Chamber Music - Townsville
August	- Grafton Street Festival - Cairns
	Rocky Roundup, Rockhampton
	National Outrigger Titles - Airlie Beach
	Hogs Breath Mooloolaba to Whitsunday Cruising
	Classic Yacht RaceXXXX Ansett Race Week at Hamilton Island (yachts)
August/ September	- 4MK Lions Sugartime Festival - Mackay
September	- Dunk Island Fosters Bill Fish Classic
	Variety Concert and Festival Awards - Cairns
	Ski Week - Great Keppel Island
	Yeppoon Tropical Pine Fest
	Billfish Classic - Dunk Island
	Whitsunday Fun Race Festival
October	-Mission Beach Aquatic Festival
	Lizard Island Black Marlin Classic
	South Molle Golf Week

Lions Cane Harvest Festival - Proserpine
Hayman Island 18 ft Skiff Race
November - Closing of Barramundi Season
Heron Island Dive Festival
Pacific Festival - Townsville
Airlie Beach Boat Show
December - Fisherman's Ball - Karumba
Nissan Billfish Bonanza - Hamilton Island

ENTRY REGULATIONS FOR OVERSEAS VISITORS

All travellers to Australia need a valid passport, and visitors of all nationalities, except New Zealand, must obtain a visa before arrival.

Australian Embassies

Canada: Australian High Commission, Suite 710, 50 O'Connor Street, Ottawa, K1P 6L2, ph (613) 236 0841.
Singapore: Australian High Commission, 25 Napier Road, Singapore 10, ph 737 9311.
UK: Australian High Commission, Australia House, The Strand, London, WC2B 4LA, ph (071) 379 4334.
US: Australian Embassy, 1601 Massachusetts Avenue NW, Washington DC, 20036, ph (202) 797 3000.

Consulate offices are also found in other cities. Consult your local telephone directory.

Before you land you will be given immigration forms as well as Customs and Agriculture declarations. As a general rule you must declare all goods of plant or animal origin. Quarantine officers will inspect these items and return them to you if no disease or pest risk is involved. If they are not prohibited, some may need to be treated before being allowed entry.

Each incoming traveller over the age of 18 is allowed duty free goods to the value of $400 plus one litre of liquor and 200 cigarettes. Do not even think of trying to bring drugs into the country - no-one is going to give our gaols a 5-star rating.

EXIT REGULATIONS

There is a departure tax of $27.00 for everyone over the age of 12 years. People taking out of the country money to the value of A$5,000 in local and/or foreign currency must file a report with Customs.

MONEY

The Australian Currency is decimal, with the Dollar as the basic unit. Notes come in a colourful array of $100, $50, $20, $10 and $5 denominations, and coins are $2, $1, 50c, 20c, 10c and 5c.

The Australian dollar tends to fluctuate, but approximate rates of exchange, which must be used as a guide only are:

CAN$1 = A$1.00
NZ$1   = A$0.94
S$1   = A$1.00
UK£1   = A$2.25
US$1   = A$1.40

Travellers cheques are the most convenient way of carrying money when travelling, and these can be exchanged at any bank, large hotel, and at any of the island resorts of the Great Barrier Reef.

Credit cards - Mastercard, Visa, American Express, Diners and the Australian/New Zealand Bankcard - are widely accepted, and most of the resorts have EFTPOS facilities.

All prices given in this book are in Australian Dollars.

COMMUNICATIONS

Telephone

The cities and towns on the mainland and the majority of the resort islands are on the main IDD/STD network, so intercity and overseas numbers can be dialled direct. The country code for Australia is 61, and in this book the area codes for each town/resort are given with the rest of the information on them. To call overseas from Australia dial 0011 + country code + area code (minus the initial 0) + local number.

Telstra Phonecards are available from pharmacies, newsagents, kiosks and tourist information centres. They come in denominations of $20, $10 and $5.

OTC Country Direct is the easiest way of making international telephone card and reverse charge (collect) calls. Upon dialling your Country Direct number you are immediately put in touch with your own country's operator who will then connect the call. Country Direct numbers are:

Canada: 0014 881 150

New Zealand: 0014 881 640

UK (BTI): 0014 881 440

USA Direct (AT&T): 0014 881 011

To obtain other Country Direct numbers, dial 0103.

Mail

Australia has an efficient postal service and the costs of sending postcards by Air Mail are:

To New Zealand 70c
Singapore 80c
Canada.....................95c
US 95c
UK $1.00

MISCELLANEOUS

Time Zones

Queensland is on Australian Eastern Time (GMT + 10) all year round - it does not change to daylight saving in the summer months like the rest of the eastern states. The result is that during the period from the end of October to the end of March there are several time zones operating in Australia instead of the usual three. This can be confusing for those who live near State borders, but remember it also affects people taking interstate flights. If you are flying somewhere and have to connect with another flight during this period, double check the times on the tickets and with the Airline to ensure you don't miss your plane.

Electricity

Domestic electricity supply through Australia is 230-250 volts, AC 50 cycles. Standard three pin plugs are fitted to domestic appliances. Appliances that use 110 volts will need a transformer. Videos in Australia operate on the PAL system.

Health

Australia has excellent health services, but they do not come cheap, especially if you are from overseas and are not covered by the Government-run Medicare. It cannot be stressed too much that travel insurance incorporating health insurance is a necessity. As someone once said about something else - don't leave home without it.

Whilst travelling in Queensland and on the Great Barrier Reef islands always wear a maximum protection sunscreen. Not only can a bad case of sunburn ruin your holiday, the effects of ultra violet rays can damage your skin.

Walking on the reef is a unique part of a Queensland holiday and is very enjoyable, but remember to wear sandshoes /runners, and treat any coral cuts carefully as they can easily lead to infection. A good method is to scrub the cut with a strong antiseptic till it bleeds (and hurts), thus ensuring that all foreign matter has been removed. If the cut should begin to swell consult a doctor. Never dive or snorkel alone, and be careful of tides and currents.

Marine Stingers

There are a few marine "nasties" that also live in tropical waters. The *Chironex*, also known as the Box Jellyfish, is present in the Rockhampton area from December to March, and in the Cairns area from late October to June. In other words, the further north, the longer the season. Stings from these creatures can be fatal. Not fatal, but still painful, are stings from Bluebottles and Pacific Man-o'War jelly blubbers.

As an unbreakable rule, if you are told by a local resident or someone working at a resort, or if there is a sign on a beach that advises people not to swim - don't!

Opposite
Millaa Millaa Falls

TRAVEL INFORMATION

HOW TO GET TO AUSTRALIA

By Air

Unless visitors have plenty of time at their disposal the only way to get to Australia is to fly, and unless you come from New Zealand, it is going to be a long flight. Always consider a stop-over, on both flights if possible, but certainly on the flight home when you will be tired after your great holiday and a ready target for jet lag. Somehow the excitement of what is in store seems to help with the outward flight.

Qantas, Australia's national carrier, has flights to Brisbane from:
  Auckland - daily except Tues and Thurs, daily via Sydney
  Christchurch - daily, with extra flights via Sydney
  Wellington - daily except Fri and Sat, daily via Sydney
  Toronto - daily via Sydney
  Vancouver - daily via Sydney
  Honolulu - daily via Sydney
  Singapore - daily
  Los Angeles - daily except Tues and Thurs, daily via Sydney
  London - daily direct and daily via Sydney
  Seoul - Thurs and Sun.

Qantas also has direct flights to Cairns from:
  Hong Kong - Wed and Sun
  Singapore - Mon, Tues
  Taipei - Tues
  Tokyo - daily.

Air New Zealand has flights to Brisbane from:
  Auckland - daily
  Christchurch - daily except Sat

Wellington - Sun, Wed
Vancouver - daily except Sat via Auckland
Honolulu - Tues, Wed, Fri and Sun via Auckland
Los Angeles - daily via Auckland.
British Airways have flights to Brisbane from:
Bangkok - Mon, Wed, Fri and Sun
London - daily via Singapore.
Cathay Pacific has direct flights from Hong Kong to Brisbane on Fri, and direct from Hong Kong to Cairns on Wed and Sat.
Singapore Airlines have direct flights to Brisbane on Mon, Thurs and Sat, and via Sydney on Wed, Fri and Sun.
United Airlines have flights to Brisbane from:
Los Angeles - daily via Sydney
San Francisco - daily via Sydney.

HOW TO GET TO THE BARRIER REEF

People who have landed in Australia at one of the eastern capital cities then have a choice of how to get to the Reef - air, rail or road.

By Air

Qantas has daily flights from Sydney, Melbourne, Adelaide, Perth, Hobart, Darwin and Canberra to Brisbane.

They also have daily flights from Brisbane to Bundaberg, Cairns, Dunk Island, Great Keppel Island, Lizard Island, Mackay, Rockhampton, Toowoomba and Townsville, and daily except Sat flights to Proserpine.

Ansett Australia have daily flights to Brisbane from Sydney, Melbourne, Adelaide, Perth, Hobart, Darwin and Canberra, although they are not all direct flights.

Ansett also have daily flights from Brisbane to Bundaberg, Cairns, Daydream Island, Hamilton Island, Long Island, Mackay, South Molle Island, Toowoomba, Townsville, and less frequent flights to Cooktown.

By Rail

The *Sunlander* leaves Brisbane on Tues, Thurs and Sat at 10am and travels through Rockhampton, Mackay, Townsville and Cairns.

The *Queenslander* leaves Brisbane on Sun at 10am and travels through Rockhampton, Mackay, Townsville and Cairns. It has first class carriages.

The *Spirit of the Tropics* leaves Brisbane on Sun at 10am and travels through Rockhampton, Mackay, Townsville and Cairns. It has economy class carriages.

More information on train travel is found in the chapters on the various destinations.

By Bus

McCafferty's and Greyhound/Pioneer are the main coach companies that operate in Australia's eastern states, so it is possible to travel with them Melbourne-Sydney-Brisbane -Cairns and points in between. But, you would have to be a dedicated coach traveller to undertake the long hike from Melbourne to Cairns, or even from Sydney to Cairns - still it is a lot cheaper than air or rail travel. The distances are listed in the following section.

By Road

If you are considering driving to Far North Queensland, it is a good idea to check out the distances involved.

Melbourne-Sydney - via the Hume Highway - 875km
via the Princes Highway - 1058km
via the Olympic Way - 961km
via Cann River/Cooma/Canberra - 1038km.
Sydney-Brisbane - via the Pacific Highway - 1000km
via the New England Highway - 1033km.

Brisbane-Rockhampton - via the Bruce Highway - 670km
via Esk and Biloela - 758km.
Rockhampton-Cairns - 1136km.
Brisbane-Mackay - via the Bruce Highway - 1020km
Mackay-Proserpine - via the Bruce Highway - 127km
Mackay-Cairns - 779km.
Brisbane-Townsville - via the Bruce Highway - 1433km.
Brisbane-Cairns - via the Bruce Highway - 1799.

TOURIST INFORMATION

Every town has an information office but in the small towns it may be part of another shop, so just keep an eye out for a large "i" sign.

Port Mackay at Sunrise.

ACCOMMODATION

On the mainland there is a wide choice of accommodation from 5-star hotels to camping areas. On the islands the choice is not so wide; **it is usually between a resort hotel and camping, with nothing in between**. And not all the islands have camping facilities. Full information on each island's available accommodation is found in the appropriate section of this book.

The resorts have many facilities for sporting activities and most are included in the accommodation fees, but usually sports that require power, eg water skiing, involve extra costs.

The Queensland National Parks & Wildlife Service (QNP&WS) controls most of the Great Barrier Reef islands, and issues the necessary camping permits for them. QNP&WS office addresses are:

Brisbane - 160 Anne Street, 4002, ph (07) 227 8197.

Rockhampton - cnr Yeppoon & Norman Roads, 4700, ph (079) 36 0511.

Gladstone - Tank Street, 4680, ph (079) 72 6055.

Capricorn Coast - Rosslyn Bay Harbour, Yeppoon, 4703, ph (079) 33 6608.

Mackay - cnr River & Wood Streets, 4740, ph (079) 51 8788.

Townsville - PO Box 5391, Townsville Mail Centre, 4810, ph (077) 74 1211.

Whitsundays - cnr Shute Harbour & Mandalay Roads, Airlie Beach, 4802, ph (079) 46 7022.

Ingham - 11 Lannercost Street, Ingham, 4850, ph (077) 76 1700.

Cardwell - 79 Victoria Street, 4816, ph (070) 66 8601.

Cairns - 10-12 McLeod Street, 4870, ph (070) 52 3092.

Mission Beach - Garners Beach Road, 4854, ph (070) 68 7183.

QNP&WS also publish leaflets on most of the islands setting out the walking tracks and camping grounds, if any.

LOCAL TRANSPORT

Transport to the Reef and the island resorts from the various coastal cities and towns will be covered in detail in each of the chapters of this book.

FOOD & DRINK

Obviously seafood is going to feature largely on any north Queensland menu, as will tropical fruit. In the section on each city you will find a list of restaurants and their specialty.

Included in the information on each island are details of the meal arrangements for the resorts. Some of the accommodation costs include meals, others don't.

Restaurants in Australia are either Licensed or BYO, although some can be both. Without going into the licensing laws of why this is so, here is a short explanation of how it will affect the diner.

A *licensed restaurant* has a wine list, and can provide beer, mixed drinks, ports, liqueurs, etc. Patrons are not allowed to provide their own drinks. A *BYO restaurant* does not have a licence to provide alcohol, so you Bring Your Own wine or beer or whatever. Glasses are provided, and a corkage fee (for opening the bottles!) may be charged, which can be per person or per bottle depending on the whim of the proprietor.

Some restaurants that do have a licence will allow you to bring your own wine (which works out cheaper), but you are not permitted to bring your own beer or spirits.

Liquor stores in Australia are called "bottle shops", and they are found everywhere.

Queensland has two main beer brands - XXXX (Fourex) and Powers, but beers from the other states, such as Tooheys, VB, Fosters and Cascade, are also found in the north.

Australian wines will also feature on all wine lists, and should be sampled by the overseas visitor. There are several extremely good wine growing areas in the country - Barossa Valley, Hunter Valley, Yarra Valley and Margaret River, to name a few.

SHOPPING

All the resort islands have stores that stock the basics of living, such as shampoo, soap, toothbrushes and toothpaste, etc, and there are usually boutiques and souvenir outlets as well. In the boutiques there is usually a good selection of sports wear, swimming costumes (locally called cozzies), board shorts, etc, but they are not exactly inexpensive.

The towns and cities on the mainland have shops and shopping centre and the usual opening hours are Mon-Fri 9.30am-5.30pm (until 9pm on either Thurs or Fri) and Sat 9.30am-4pm. In the tourist areas the shops are usually open every day and for longer hours.

Toy kangaroos and koalas are high on everyone's shopping list, and are available everywhere. Everything Aboriginal is popular and items are found in all centres. The most sought after articles, though, are opals.

When buying opals there are a few terms you should be familiar with:

Solid Opal - this is the most valuable, and good for investment purposes. The more colourful and complete, the greater its value.

Doublet - this is slices of opal glued together, and is of medium value. It has no investment value.

Triples - this is slices of opal covered with quartz, perspex or glass, and is the least expensive. It has no investment value.

If your pocket can't stretch as far as a solid opal, but you still would like a piece of opal jewellery, remember that anything that is glued can come unstuck, and that condensation can form under perspex or glass. The less expensive types of opal are not suitable for rings, unless you are going to remember to take it off every time you wash your hands.

Australia produces more than 90% of the world's opals, and the three main areas where they are found are Lightning Ridge which produces the Black Opal; Quilpie, where the ueensland Bounder Opal originates; and Coober Pedy, which has the White or Milk Opal.

THE CAPRICORN COAST

T he Capricorn Coast main area begins at the town of Joskeleigh in the south and reaches north to the forests and national parks of Byfield. The main town on the coast is Yeppoon, and the main city in the area is Rockhampton, 41km from the coast.

Rockhampton airport is the departure point for flights to the nearby islands of the Reef.

ROCKHAMPTON

Gateway to the Capricorn Coast, Rockhampton is 671km north of Brisbane, on the Tropic of Capricorn. The city is situated on the Fitzroy River, about 41km from the coast.

Rocky is the heart of the beef cattle country. The main breeds are Santa Gertrudis, Hereford, Braford and Brahman. Rockhampton also has two flour mills that process wheat from the Central Highlands around Emerald.

CLIMATE

Average temperatures: January max 31C (88F) - min 22C (72F); July max 23C (73F) - min 9C (48F). Most rain falls between December and March - approximately 500mm.

HOW TO GET THERE

By Air

Qantas and *Ansett Australia* have several flights daily from Brisbane to Rockhampton, and these flights connect with flights from the other capital cities.

By Bus

McCafferty's and Greyhound/Pioneer stop at Rockhampton on their daily Brisbane-North Queensland routes.

By Rail

The *Spirit of Capricorn* leaves Brisbane daily at 8.25am, arriving in Rocky at 5.50pm. There is an extra service on Wed and Sun leaving at 8.30pm and arriving at 6am the following day.
The *Sunlander* leaves Brisbane at 10am on Tues, Thurs and Sat, arriving in Rocky at 9.05pm.
The *Queenslander* leaves Brisbane on Sun at 10am and arrives in Rockhampton at 8.30pm.
The *Spirit of the Tropics* leaves Brisbane at 3.40pm on Thurs and arrives in Rockhampton at 2.15am Fri.

By Car

From Brisbane, via the Bruce Highway, is 670km; inland via Esk and Biloela is 795km.
Rockhampton is 1413km south of Cairns.

TOURIST INFORMATION

The Capricorn Information Centre is in Curtis Park, Gladstone Road, ph (079) 272 055, adjacent to the Tropic of Capricorn Spire. The office is open seven days a week.

ACCOMMODATION

Rockhampton has no shortage of motels, and there are plenty of the older style hotels near the city centre. Here is a selection with prices for a double room per night, which should be used as a guide only. The telephone area code is 079.

Country Comfort Inn, 86 Victoria Parade, ph 279 933 - 76 units, licensed restaurant, swimming pool - $92.

Centre Point Motor Inn, 131 George Street, ph 278 844 - 34 units, licensed restaurant, swimming pool - $74.

Albert Court Motel, cnr Albert & Alma Streets, ph 277 433 - 44 units, licensed restaurant (closed Sunday), swimming pool - $65.

Country Lodge Motor Inn, 112 Gladstone Road, ph 278 866 - 32 units, licensed restaurant, swimming pool - $65.

Central Park Motel, 224 Murray Street, ph 272 333 - 25 units, licensed restaurant, swimming pool - $65.

Archer Park Motel, 39 Albert Street, ph 279 266 - 16 units, licensed restaurant (closed Sun), swimming pool - $63.

Golden Fountain Motel, 166 Gladstone Road, ph 271 055 - 31 units, swimming pool - $55.

Duthies Leichhardt Motel, cnr Denham & Bolsover Streets, ph 276 733 - 120 units, restaurant and bistro - $48.

Caravan Parks

Tropical Wanderer Caravan Village, 394 Yaamba Road, North Rockhampton, ph 263 822 - powered sites $17, non-powered sites $12; cabins $35; ensuite cabins $48; Villas $48.

Ramblers Motel/Park, Yaamba Road (opposite Rockhampton Shopping Fair, ph 282 084 - powered sites $14; non-powered sites $12; cabins $33; ensuite cabins $38; villas $42.

Southside Caravan Village, Lower Dawson Road, ph 273 013 - powered sites $16; non-powered suites $12; cabins $32; ensuite cabins $38; villas $44.

Riverside Caravan Park (Municipal), Reaney Street, North Rockhampton, ph 223 779 - powered sites $12; non-powered sites $9.

Country Club Caravan Park, Bruce Highway, North Rockhampton, ph 361 022 - powered sites $10, non-powered sites $8; villas $35.

EATING OUT

Most of the hotels serve casual counter meals, and the steaks in Rocky are particularly large, as this is the heart of the cattle country.

The hotels, and several motels, also have licensed restaurants, but here are some eateries for you to try.

Italian Graffiti, 147 Musgrave Street, ph 226 322 - Italian bistro, open daily - takeaway available.

Malaysia Hut Restaurant, 7 Wandal Road, ph 277 511 - open daily, banquets available, children welcome.

Tropical Wanderer Restaurant, 394 Yaamba Road, ph 282 621 - a la carte, open Mon-Sat.

Wintersun Restaurant, Bruce Highway, ph 288 722 - bistro open Mon-Sat.

For the kids, or people in a hurry, *McDonald's* is at the corner of Fitzroy and George Streets, ph 224 920, and *Hungry Jack's* is on the corner of High Street and Bruce Highway, ph 261 533.

Rockhampton Anzac Club, at 8 Archer Street, has the *Garden Inn Restaurant*, entertainment, and the usual poker machines. Visitors are welcome.

ENTERTAINMENT

Rockhampton has a three cinema complex and indoor and outdoor concert venues.

There are three nightclubs in the city -

Flamingo's, cnr Quay and Williams Streets

Strutters Uptown, cnr East and Williams Streets

Pinocchio's Nite Club, 189 East and William Streets.

The *Pilbeam Theatre and Art Gallery* in Victoria Parade are the cultural centre of Rocky. The Art Gallery has an extensive collection of Australian paintings, pottery and sculpture, and is open Mon-Fri 10am-4pm, Wed also 7-8.30pm and Sun 2-4pm. The Pilbeam Theatre attracts regular performances by national and international artists.

Ask at the tourist information office for details of current entertainment programs at hotels, clubs, etc.

SHOPPING

No-one would ever describe Rockhampton as a shopping capital, but the Shopping Fair has recently been refurbished. It has a Big W, two supermarkets, over 100 specialty shops, a food court, Sizzlers and another licensed restaurant.

The City Heart Mall has local art and craft markets on Saturdays.

SIGHTSEEING

Rockhampton was first settled in the 1850s by Charles and William Archer. Today, historic *Quay Street* contains over 20 buildings that have been classified by the National Trust.

The city is the commercial and administrative centre of central Queensland. Its wide streets are lined with trees and solid buildings, indicating a prosperity dating back to the early days. The Australian Estate Co Ltd offices were built in 1861, and the Customs House in 1901. It has a handsome copper dome and a striking semi-circular portico.

Queens Wharf is all that remains of the quays of the port that was very busy until silt caused the demise of the river trade.

St Joseph's Cathedral, cnr Murray and William Streets, and *St Paul's Anglican Cathedral* are both built in Gothic style from local sandstone.

The *Royal Arcade* was built in 1889 as a theatre with a special feature - the roof could be opened on hot nights.

The *Botanic Gardens* in Spencer Street are reputed to be one of the finest tropical gardens in Australia. Spreading over 4ha, they contain many native and exotic trees, ferns and shrubs, as well as a large walk-in aviary, orchid and fern house, and a small Australian Zoo that includes its own Koala Park. A part of a sister city agreement with Ibusuki City in Japan, separate Japanese Gardens were created in 1982.

St Aubin's Village, Canoona Road near the airport, consists of one of Rockhampton's oldest houses, and a number of gift shops specialising in cottage industries.

Callaghan Park Racecourse is Queensland's premier provincial racetrack. Thursday night has greyhound racing, Saturday evening has harness racing, and Saturday afternoon it is the gallopers' turn.

Old Glenmore Homestead, Belmont Road, North Rockhampton, is a 130-year-old complex consisting of a log cabin, slab cottage and an adobe house. Old Glenmore holds

Queensland's first Historic Inn Licence, so visitors can sample some of the State's best fermented beverages in this pleasant old world setting. The homestead is open to all Sun 11am-3pm only, and if you are not into alcohol during the day you can sample their tea and damper. Glenmore is also open for evening dinners and entertainment, but it is absolutely essential that you book ahead on (079) 36 1033.

On the Bruce Highway, 23km north of the city is the turn-off to **The Caves**. There are two privately owned cave systems, each with good examples of ancient geological formations. Both are open seven days. Guided tours of the award winning *Olsen's Capricorn Caverns* are available, with the option of adventure caving on request, ph (079) 342 883.

Cammoo Caves have a sign-posted self-guiding tour of the well-lit cavern, with audio station commentaries positioned throughout. For opening times and entry fees phone (079) 342 774.

The *Dreamtime Cultural Centre* is a large Aboriginal and Torres Strait Islander centre, and is on the Bruce Highway 7km north of Rockhampton opposite the turn-off to Yeppoon. It is open daily 10am-5pm, with tours at 11am and 2pm and Aboriginal dancing at 12.30pm Mon-Fri.

Rockhampton Heritage Village is 20km north of Rockhampton, although there are plans to relocate it in Parkhurst. Attractions include a blacksmith's shop, wheel wrighting, dairy, fully furnished slab cottage, pioneering tools, vintage cars, horse-drawn vehicles, hall of clocks and a kiosk. Tours are conducted daily, and there are working demonstrations on the last Sunday of each month. Open daily.

WEST OF ROCKHAMPTON

Mount Hay Gemstone Tourist Park is 40km from Rockhampton on the Capricorn Highway. There you can fossick for 120 million-year-old Thundereggs. When the eggs are cut, in the gemstone factory on the premises, beautiful agate patterns are exposed. Facilities here also include a swimming pool, craft and gift shop, barbecue facilities, ensuite cabins ($10 per person per night) and caravan sites (powered $10; non-powered $7). For more information phone (079) 347 183.

The historic township of *Mount Morgan* is 38km south-west of Rockhampton, and there you can tour through a 100-year-old mining town that is the real thing, not a reconstruction. Mt Morgan was listed as a Heritage Town by the Australian Heritage Commission in 1980, and by the National Trust of Queensland in 1981. The Museum on Morgan Street, ph (079) 382 122, traces the history of the fabulously rich mine, and is open Mon-Sat 10am-1pm, Sun 10am-4pm. Inspections of the Silver Wattle Gold Mine, which are by bus tour only, leave from the Tour Office at 12.50pm and from the Museum at 1pm, ph (079) 381 081.

The historic *Mount Morgan Railway Station* is the departure point for fettler's trolley rides daily, and the historic train ride on Saturdays, ph (079) 382 312.

Belgamba Cottage offers guided bush walks of the Bouldercombe Gorge Reserve, and has self-contained accommodation, ph (079) 38 1818.

SPORT

Rockhampton has all the usual facilities you would expect of a town of its size. To get to the beach, though, you have to drive 45km to the Capricorn Coast.

Capricorn Reef Diving, ph (079) 227 720, offer 5-day open water certificate PADI course. The classroom is in Rockhampton, then 4 dives on the Keppel Island Group - $385.

TOURS

Rothery's Day Tours, ph (079) 222 400, offer tours of the city and to the Capricorn Coast, Koorana Crocodile Farm, Cooberrie Park, The Caves, Dreamtime Culture Centre.

Silver Wattle Tours, 38 Central Street, ph (079) 381 081, travel to see huge Shale Caves, dinosaur footprints, and the historic gold/copper mine, leaving at 9.30am and 12.50pm daily - $18.50 adult, $10 child.

CAPRICORN HIGHLANDS

The highlands stretch from the Carnarvon to Clermont, from Blackwater to Jericho, and the region is one of the most diverse and productive areas in the country. Coal, sapphires, cattle, sheep, wheat, sunflower, sorghum and cotton are but a few of the riches produced from around here. The Emerald Irrigation Scheme, along with the Fairbairn Dam, has increased rural productivity tenfold in the heart of the Highlands.

A visit to this area can be a rewarding experience. The Carnarvon Gorge offers a breath-taking view of scenery, lush vegetation, Aboriginal art and escorted bush walks. The town of *Springsure* has the famous Virgin Rock, and from *Emerald*, the hub of the Central Highlands, you can join a conducted tour of the Gregory Coal Mine. Travelling through *Capella* brings you to the township of *Clermont*, which was almost completely destroyed by a flood in 1916. The remaining buildings were moved to the present location with the aid of a huge steam engine which has been preserved as a memorial in the centre of the town.

A National Park at *Blackdown Tablelands* offers camping facilities and good views.

After crossing the Drummond Range, the country opens out into Queensland's vast grazing lands, and towns like *Alpha* and *Jericho* are becoming increasingly popular stopovers for people visiting this outback area. It has become even more so since the opening in 1988 of the Stockman's Hall of Fame at *Longreach*.

The Central Queensland gem fields are a popular tourist spot in the Capricorn Region, and visitors come for a chance to "stub their toe on a sapphire". Towns such as *Anakie, Sapphire, Rubyvale* and the *Willows Gemfields* must be experienced to be fully appreciated. In Rubyvale you can visit a walk-in mine, called Bobby Dazzler, which has guided tours and is open daily 8am-6pm. For more information phone (079) 854 170.

LADY ELLIOT ISLAND

The most southerly of the islands of the Great Barrier Reef, Lady Elliot has an area of 0.42 sq km and has been nicknamed Queensland's "Shipwreck Island". This name is not unwarranted as the wrecks of many ships can be seen littered around the island's shores. The first was probably in 1851, the *Bolton Abbey* a cargo ship, and the latest was possibly the *Tenggara II* which hit the reef in April, 1989.

The island is also popular with bird watchers as 57 species are known to flock here, with more than 200,000 birds nesting here during the summer. Sea turtles also nest on Lady Elliot.

Lady Elliot is a favourite with divers, as it is an unspoilt coral cay that is actually part of the reef, and you can snorkel or dive straight from the beach.

HOW TO GET THERE

By Air

The island has an airstrip and Sunset Airlines fly daily from Bundaberg to Lady Elliot. Bookings and enquiries should be made to Sunstate Travel Centre, ph (071) 522 322.

These flights can be taken by resort guests, who get a discounted fare, or by day-trippers for whom the around $135 fare includes the return flights, a picnic lunch, reef walking and snorkelling.

It only takes about an hour to walk around the entire island, and it is one of the least commercialised.

ACCOMMODATION

The **Resort**, ph (071) 532 485, is located on the beach front, and is rated at 2-Star. It has a restaurant, cocktail bar, swimming pool, entertainment, novelty golf course, dive shop, resort shop, poolside bar and bistro, Reef education centre, glass bottom boat, baby sitting, snorkelling, scuba courses, guided eco tours, charter fishing boat, and a tour desk.

Units have private facilities, fans, balcony and maid service.

Prices per person, twin share, are:

Reef Unit (Garden) - $138.00, extra night $138.00

Reef Unit (Beachfront) - $148.00, extra night $148.00

A child sharing with 2 adults is half price.

Tariff includes accommodation, dinner, breakfast and most activities.

Maximum occupancy of each unit is 4 persons (a child is counted as a person).

Reservations can be made through Sunstate Travel, ph (071) 522 322, or by writing to Lady Elliot Resort, PO Box 206, Torquay, Hervey Bay, Qld, 4655.

Credit cards accepted: Visa, MasterCard, Bankcard, American Express, Diners Club, JCB.

Accommodation is also available in 10 tent/cabins - they look like tents, but are permanent structures - for $99 per person per night. Reservations for these can also be made through Sunstate Travel.

DIVING

There are ten excellent diving sites that include Lighthouse Bommie, Coral Gardens, Moiri and Shark Pool. Visibility ranges from 80 to 25 to 50 metres. This island is also paradise for those who like exploring shipwrecks.

All equipment can be hired from the resort, and five day certificate courses are available for around $400. Shore dives cost around $25, boat dives around $30 and night dives around $40.

LADY MUSGRAVE ISLAND

Lady Musgrave Island is part of the Capricorn Bunker Group, and is about 100km north-east of Bundaberg. It is a true coral cay, approximately 18ha in area, and rests on the edge of a huge coral lagoon that measures some eight kilometres in circumference and covers an area of around 1192ha. The lagoon is one of very few on the Reef that ships can enter, making the island very popular with the yachting fraternity. Lady Musgrave is a National and Marine Park, and an unspoilt section of the Great Barrier Reef.

HOW TO GET THERE

MV *Lady Musgrave* is a catamaran that sails from Port Bundaberg at 8.30am on Tues, Thurs, Sat and Sun, with extra services during school holidays. Even so, it is always advisable to book well ahead through Lady Musgrave Barrier Reef Cruises, 1 Quay Street, Bundaberg, ph (071) 529 011. The trip out to the island takes about 2 1/2 hours, and passengers are allowed four hours on the island.

On reaching the island passengers are transferred to the semi-submersible for some coral viewing, and on returning to the catamaran a visit is made to the underwater observatory. Lunch is then served and afterwards passengers are taken ashore to explore the island. Snorkelling gear is provided for the day.

The cruise connects with a bus service that operates from Bundaberg and Bargara, which costs $6 return. The cruise costs around $100.

This cruise can also be used for people wishing to camp on Lady Musgrave.

ACCOMMODATION

There is absolutely no choice in this regard, if you wish to stay on Lady Musgrave Island you have to camp. There are staff on-site, toilets and walking trails, and that is it. You have to first obtain a camping permit from the QNP&WS, and fees are $2/person/night, $10/site/night for a family group with no more than 2 people over 15 years.

DIVING

The island is reputedly one of the finest dive sites on the Great Barrier Reef, and is home to around 1200 species of fish and 350 varieties of corals. The lagoon is reasonably shallow, allowing longer dives to be undertaken.

MV *Lady Musgrave* always has qualified diving instructors on board for the inexperienced, but they can also head the certified divers in the best direction to get the most out of their trip.

HERON ISLAND

The island is about 72km east of Gladstone, roughly 100km from Rockhampton, and has an area of 19ha. It is a true coral cay that sits on the Tropic of Capricorn, surrounded by 24 sq km of reef.

It is possible to walk around the island in less than half an hour, and there is usually an organised beach and reef walk every day. Heron's eastern end has a track system that leads through dense pisonia forest and open grassy shrubland, with information posts along the way. In the summer months be sure to stay on the track, or you could destroy one of the many shearwater burrows that honeycomb the island.

The survey vessel *Fly* was the first to record the existence of Heron Island during its voyage of 1843. The captain named the island after the many reef herons, which are now known as reef egrets. Nothing much is recorded of visitors to the islands until around 1910 when bird-watchers and other naturalists came to explore. These groups did not usually have their bases on Heron, so their visits were only brief sojourns.

In the mid 1920s a canning factory was built where the resort office now stands, and turtle harvesting began. By the end of the decade the supply of turtles had dwindled and industry here ceased, although some turtles were caught here and sent south right up until they were declared a protected species in 1950. The clumsy creatures still come to Heron to lay their eggs.

In 1932, the canning factory was converted into a resort by Cristian Poulsen, and in 1936 he was granted the special lease on which the resort is built. Many facilities were added to the resort, and a regular flying-boat service was established before Poulsen disappeared from a dinghy near the island in 1947. The resort remained in the family until 1974.

The Heron Island research station commenced operations in 1951 and has an international reputation for coral reef research and education. In 1943 a national park was declared on Heron Island, and in 1974 Queensland's first marine national park was declared over Heron and Wistari Reefs. In 1979 the Capricornia section of the Great Barrier Reef Marine Park was declared under new federal government legislation.

HOW TO GET THERE

Unfortunately, due to its distance from the mainland, Heron Island is one of the most expensive islands to visit.

By Air

Lloyd's Helicopter Service, ph (079) 781 177, fly from Gladstone to Heron Island, and the trip takes about 30 minutes. They don't have a regular schedule, but will meet flights into Gladstone to transfer passengers to the island. Obviously it is best to contact them before you arrive in Gladstone. Fares are $212 one-way, $353 return, with some standby seats at $97 one-way.

By Sea

The catamaran *Reef Adventurer* makes the trip from Gladstone to Heron in a little under two hours, but it can be a very choppy trip, so make sure you have some seasickness pills. Fares are $65 one-way, $130 return (adult); $32.50 one-way, $65 return (child). Bookings can be made through Gladstone Travel World, ph (079) 727 277; Hervey World Travel, ph (079) 723 488; and Gladstone Travel Land, ph (079) 722 288. Reduced standby fares are also available on the *Reef Adventurer*.

ACCOMMODATION

Heron Island has lodges and suites, and prices for both include all meals. There are 26 lodge rooms that offer shared rooms and shared bathroom and toilet facilities. The tariff is $150 per person/bed, and the rooms have beds for three or four people, so in peak periods it may be necessary to share a room with strangers.

The **Resort** has three types of suites - Reef at $197 per person, twin share; Heron at $215 per person, twin share; and Point at $260 per person, twin share. Children 3-14 years are half price. As mentioned previously, these prices include all meals, and most activities. Maximum occupancy for the suites is 4 persons (a child is counted as one person).

Resort facilities are: restaurant, cocktail bar, coffee shop, tennis court, games room, two swimming pools, babysitting, discotheque, entertainment, reef walks, jumbo outdoor chess, dive shop, resort shop, SCUBA courses, Snorkelling, Kids Klub during school holiday and Semi-submersible reef viewer.

Rooms have private facilities, tea and coffee making facilities, refrigerator, mini bar on request, ceiling fans, daily cleaning service and inter-connecting rooms.

Credit cards accepted: Visa, MasterCard, Bankcard, American Express, JCB.

DIVING

At other islands on the Reef it is sometimes necessary to travel 70 or 80 km for scuba diving and snorkelling, but at Heron the

Reef is at the foot of the white sandy beaches.

One of the most spectacular diving sites is the well-known Heron Bommie, a head of hard coral rising more than 18m from the seabed that is home to all kinds of fish and marine life, including two friendly Moral Eels named Harry and Fang.

All equipment can be hired from the resort's dive shop, and the six-day certificate diving course costs around $375.00. Day dives, including all equipment, cost around $40.

Heron hosts a week-long Dive Festival in November each year, when divers from all over the world gather to swap knowledge and experience. There are those who think that this island rates highly among the world's premier dive locations.

GREAT KEPPEL ISLAND

The Keppel Island group of 30 islands is situated 55km from Rockhampton, and 15km east of Rosslyn Bay on the Capricorn Coast. Great Keppel is the only island in the group to have been developed, and this is because of its permanent water supply as well as its size (14 sq km).

Some islands in the group are national parks - North Keppel, Miall, Middle, Halfway, Humpy and Peak - where camping is permitted, but numbers are limited. All drinking water has to be taken to these islands, but some have water for washing, and some have toilets, but it is best to get full information from the QNP&WS office on the corner of Yeppoon and Norman Roads, North Rockhampton, ph (079) 360 511, when applying for a camping permit. It is also wise to check on the fishing regulations for the area you are going to visit.

The Middle Island Underwater Observatory is a popular attraction. It is surrounded by natural coral, and the area teems with marine life of every type imaginable. A sunken wreck nearby also provides a haven for fish, sea snakes, turtles and a school of huge cod.

Pumpkin Island is privately owned, and has five cabins

available for occupation, ph (079) 392 431. Prices range from $100 per day, and visitors must supply their own linen and all food.

Great Keppel

In May 1770 Captain Cook sailed past Great Keppel and named it after Admiral Augustus Keppel, who later became the First Lord of the Admiralty.

A naturalist from the *Rattlesnake* is given the credit of being the first European to visit the island when he came ashore in 1847, but the Woppabura Aboriginal people had been living there for over 4,500 years. They called the island Wapparaburra, the name now belonging to the cabin/camping resort.

The first European settlers arrived in 1906, but they could not live happily with the Aborigines and in fact treated them very badly. The Leeke family moved to the island in the 1920s and grazed sheep there until the 1940s. There name is remembered in Leeke's Beach and Leeke's Creek, and the restored Homestead is where they lived. The resort opened in 1967, and is now operated by Qantas.

Although not situated on the Reef, Great Keppel is the gateway to the Outer Reef and North West Island, the largest coral cay in the Great Barrier Reef. It is a major breeding ground for Green Turtles, White Capped Noddy Terns, Wedge Tailed Shearwaters and Olive Head Sea Snakes.

Day trips from Great Keppel to the Outer Reef are available on the *Capricorn Reefseeker*, run by Capricorn Cruises, ph (079) 336 744.

HOW TO GET THERE

By Air

Qantas has two flights daily from Rockhampton to Great Keppel Island. Flights from other cities connect with these flights.

ROCKHAMPTON

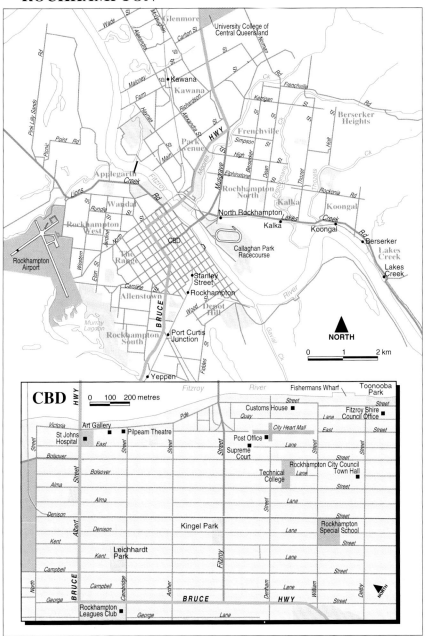

ROCKHAMPTON-YEPPOON

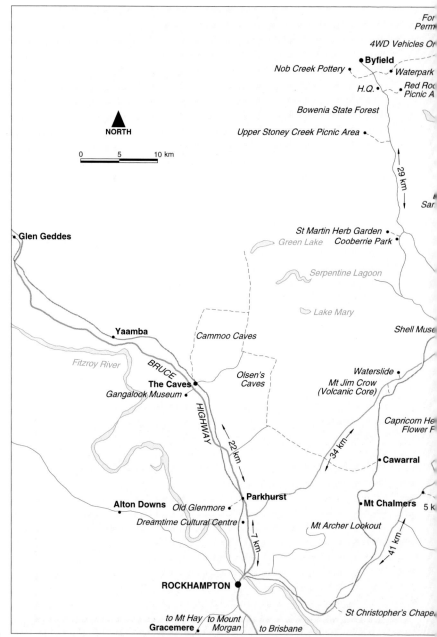

For
Perm

4WD Vehicles On

Byfield

Nob Creek Pottery • • Waterpark

H.Q. • • Red Roc
Picnic A

Bowenia State Forest

Upper Stoney Creek Picnic Area •

NORTH

0   5   10 km

29 km

Sar

Glen Geddes •

St Martin Herb Garden •
Green Lake   Cooberrie Park •

Serpentine Lagoon

Lake Mary

Yaamba •

Cammoo Caves

Shell Muse

Fitzroy River

BRUCE

Waterslide •
Mt Jim Crow
(Volcanic Core)

The Caves •
Gangalook Museum •

Olsen's
Caves

HIGHWAY

22 km

34 km

Capricorn He
Flower F

• **Cawarral**

Alton Downs •
Old Glenmore •

Parkhurst

• **Mt Chalmers**   5 k

Dreamtime Cultural Centre •

Mt Archer Lookout

41 km

7 km

ROCKHAMPTON •

to Mt Hay / to Mount   St Christopher's Chape
Gracemere •   Morgan   to Brisbane

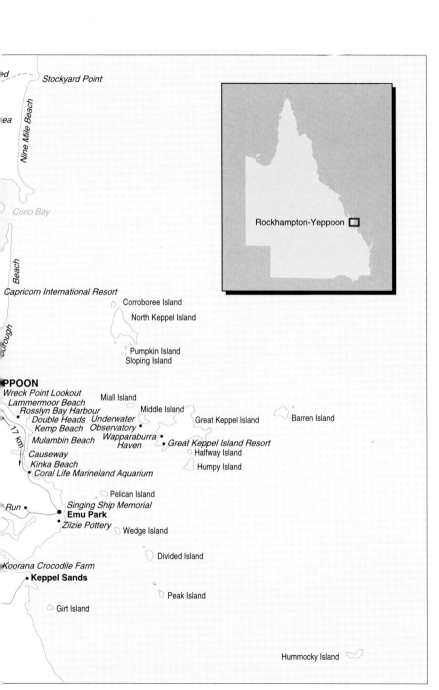

Stockyard Point

Nine Mile Beach

Corio Bay

Beach

Capricorn International Resort

Corroboree Island

North Keppel Island

Pumpkin Island
Sloping Island

Rockhampton-Yeppoon

PPOON
Wreck Point Lookout   Miall Island
Lammermoor Beach   Middle Island
Rosslyn Bay Harbour
Double Heads Underwater   Great Keppel Island   Barren Island
Kemp Beach   Observatory
Mulambin Beach   Wapparaburra   Great Keppel Island Resort
Causeway   Haven   Halfway Island
Kinka Beach   Humpy Island
Coral Life Marineland Aquarium

Pelican Island
Singing Ship Memorial
Run   **Emu Park**
Zilzie Pottery   Wedge Island

Divided Island

Koorana Crocodile Farm
Keppel Sands

Peak Island

Girt Island

Hummocky Island

17 km

MACKAY

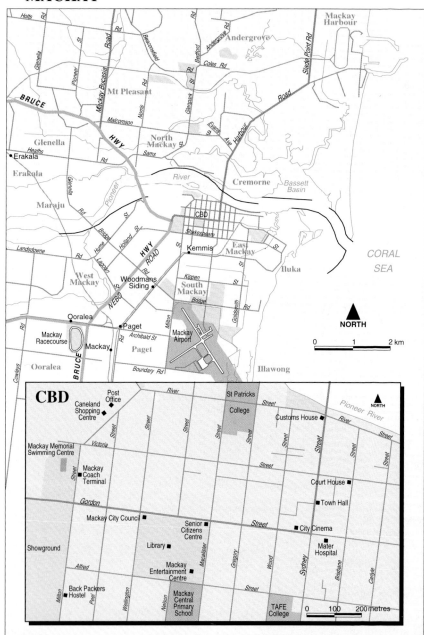

By Sea

Ferries leave from Rosslyn Bay Harbour, south of Yeppoon. Capricorn Cruises have the *Spirit of Keppel* which sails from the bay at 9.15am, 11am and 3.30pm and costs $24.00 return. Or, you could use the day cruise mentioned above to get to the island. It departs 9am, returns at 4.30pm and costs $35.00. It is more expensive, but remember that an Outer Reef cruise is included.

The *Keppel Princess*, ph (079) 336 865, seats 250 and leaves from Rosslyn Bay. Tickets are available from the Rosslyn Bay Kiosk and the return fare is $15.00 adult, $35 family.

The smaller and faster *Australis*, ph (079) 336 865, departs Rosslyn Bay Commercial Wharf every day at 9am and 11am and return fares are $20 adult, $50 family (2 adults + 2 children).

If you are staying in Rockhampton, check with the ferry company about connecting bus services to Rosslyn Bay, or contact Rothery's, ph (079) 224 320, or Young's Bus Service, ph (079) 223 813.

Visitors that have their own transport can enquire about long-term parking at Kempsea Car Park, ph (079) 336 670, which is north of the harbour turn-off, on the main road, and has complimentary transport from there to the wharf.

ACCOMMODATION

The **Resort** has over 190 units, labelled Garden, Beachfront or Ocean View. The Garden and Beachfront are rated 3-star, and the new Ocean View units are 4-star.

Resort facilities are: nightclub, live entertainment, restaurants, bars, four swimming pools, spa, kids' club, games room, squash, tennis courts, laundry/ironing, quick snack bar, fishing, babysitting, tube rides, golf, tandem-skydiving, cricket, waterskiing, parasailing, baseball, snorkelling, sailboarding, catamaran sailing, beach volleyball, SCUBA diving, cruising and coral-viewing, Barrier Reef trips, EFTPOS.

Unit facilities are: tea and coffee making facilities, refrigerator, ceiling fans (Garden and Beachfront) air-conditioning (Ocean View), colour TV, in-house movies, IDD/STD telephone, radio, inter-connecting rooms, daily cleaning service.

Tariffs for one night per person/twin share are:

Garden - $124 adult (child 3-14 sharing with 2 adults - free)

Beachfront - $155 adult (child - as above)

Ocean View - $155 adult (child - as above).

Cheaper rates are available for longer stays.

The above rates are room only, but there is a meal option, with costs for one night as follows:

Breakfast - $18 adult, $9 child

Breakfast and Dinner - $47 adult, $24 child

Full Board - $60 adult, $28 child.

Additional to the Tariff are: Barrier Reef trips, boom netting, cruising and coral viewing, deserted island drop-off, dinghies with outboards, fishing and yacht charters, island waterways cruise, kids campout (children 5-14 years), masseuse, scuba diving courses, scuba diving trips to the Great Barrier Reef, sunset cruise, tandem skydiving, tube rides, underwater observatory, waterskiing.

Reservations can be made through Australian Resorts, ph 008 812 525 (7 days), from overseas ph (+ 61 7) 360 2444, or through any Qantas office. The Resort address is Great Keppel Island Resort, CMB, Great Keppel Island, Qld, 4702, ph (079) 395 044, fax (079) 391 775.

Credit cards accepted: Visa, MasterCard, Bankcard, Diners Club, American Express, JCB.

Wapparaburra Haven Cabin & Camping Resort, ph (079) 391 907, fax (079) 393 464, have 6-berth cabins with full kitchen facilities, laundry and bedding, but shared bathrooms - $75 for two people, $15 for each additional person.

There are also 5-berth pre-erected tents that have mattresses and cost $15 per person. There is under-cover communal cooking and washing-up facilities, a refrigerator and barbecue, but no kitchen utensils.

And lastly, there are tent sites on a shaded area close to the beach for $9 per person.

Resort facilities include kiosk, gift shop, licensed restaurant, dive shop, jet ski and water sports hire.

Adjacent to Wapparaburra is **Great Keppel Island Kamp-Out**, ph (079) 392 131. It also has pre-erected tents, but a different price schedule. It is aimed at the 18 to 35 age bracket, and costs $69 per person for twin share accommodation, full board, and activities such as water sports, video nights and parties. There is even wine included with dinner. Linen is supplied, but it is BYO towels. Sometimes stand-by rates are possible - 2 days/1 night for $49.00.

Keppel Lodge, ph (079) 394 251, has four motel units that sleep up to 5 people, with private facilities, for $80 a double or twin, plus $25 for each additional person, or $12.50 for children under 12. There is a communal lounge, a good kitchen, and an outside barbecue area.

Great Keppel YHA Hostel, ph (079) 394 341, is behind the Wapparaburra Kiosk, and has two 16-bed dormitories in the main building, with a kitchen, bathrooms and a laundry. It also has two separate eight-bed units with bathrooms. Tariffs are $14 per bed (dorm), $16 per bed (unit), $1 extra for non-members. Bookings can be made direct, through Rockhampton YHA, ph (079) 275 288, or YHA in Brisbane.

Tent and cabin accommodation packages, which include boat transfers and a few other extras, can be organised through *Keppel Haven*, Rosslyn Bay Harbour, Yeppoon, ph (079) 336 744

EATING OUT

The *Wapparaburra Kiosk*, open daily 8am-6pm, stocks basic supplies, including fruit and vegetables, and also offers sandwiches, hamburgers and hot dogs. Next door is the *Reef Bar*, which offers very reasonably-priced meals, with special $10 nights on Wednesday and Saturday.

Between the Resort and Wapparaburra is the *Shell House*, where you can get really tasty Devonshire tea for around $5, or pick up some scones and cakes for afternoon tea at home. The place has, of course, a good shell collection, and is owned by a gem of information on the history of the island.

Nearby is *Island Pizza*, which also sells hot dogs, subs and pasta, all at reasonable prices.

DIVING

A glance at a map will show that the Great Barrier Reef is a long way from the mainland at this point, but there is some good diving closer to Great Keppel Island. Bald Rock and Man & Wife Rocks are popular diving venues, and between the southern end of Halfway Island and Middle Island Reef there is some good coral.

If the weather is calm there is good diving at Parker's Bombora, off the south-eastern tip of Great Keppel. It begins in water about 20m deep and is encircled by sea ferns, sponges, coral and hundreds of fish.

Typical tropical aspect of the city of Mackay.

The **outer islands** of the Keppel group, particularly **Barren Island**, have deeper and clearer water than Great Keppel, so larger species of sea life are encountered, like turtles and manta rays.

All diving gear can be hired from the accommodation outlets on Great Keppel, or you can be organised on the mainland (*see Rockhampton section*).

YEPPOON

A modern town with a population of over 10,000, Yeppoon nestles beside pineapple covered hills on the shores of Keppel Bay. Palms and pines line the main street, and shady trees continue to line to road to Rockhampton. There is a 4m difference between high and low tide, so trawlers, yachts and dinghies are left high and dry.

Yeppoon is the main town on the Capricorn Coast, and is one of the largest and fastest growing coastal communities in Queensland. It is a popular holiday spot, offering access to more than 40km of safe beaches.

HOW TO GET THERE

Young's Coaches travel from the corner of Denham & Bolsover Streets, Rockhampton to Yeppoon at the following times:
Mon-Fri - 6.10am, 7.45am, 8.45am, 10am, 2pm, 3.30pm, 4.30pm, 5.20pm, 6.15pm
Sat - 7.45am, 12.15pm, 3.30pm
Sun - 7.45am, 10am, 3.30pm
and the trip takes 45 minutes. Young's also have services to Rosslyn Bay, Emu Park and Keppel Sands.

If you have your own transport, the turn-off from the Bruce Highway for Yeppoon is just north of Rockhampton, opposite the Dreamtime Cultural Centre.

TOURIST INFORMATION

The Capricorn Coast Tourist Organisation has an office at the roundabout as you drive into town (you can't miss it!) and it is open daily 9am-5pm, ph (079) 394 888.

ACCOMMODATION

Here is a selection of available accommodation, with prices for a double room per night, which should be used as a guide only. The telephone area code is 079.

Capricorn International Resort, Farnborough Road, ph 395 111 - licensed restaurant, cocktail bar, swimming pool, sauna, gymnasium, tennis golf, mini golf, archery, bowls, catamaran sailing, horse riding, scuba diving, volleyball, wind surfing, kids kapers - hotel section $145, apartment section - $180.

Bayview Tower Motel, cnr Adelaide & Normanby Streets, ph 394 500 - 34 units, licensed restaurant, swimming pool, spa, sauna - $68-96.

Driftwood Motel, 7 Todd Avenue, ph 392 446 - 9 units, swimming pool, barbecue facilities - $45-60.

Sail Inn Motel, 19 James Street, ph 391 130 - 9 units, barbecue facilities - $38-50.

Strand Hotel/Motel, cnr Normanby Street & Anzac Parade, ph 391 301 - 15 units, swimming pool - $45.

EATING OUT

There are several restaurants in the Capricorn International Resort, or you could try some of the following.

Happy Sun Chinese Restaurant, 34 James Street, ph 393 323 - open daily with a smorgasbord dine-in on Sunday.

Chain and Anchor Restaurant, Keppel Bay Sailing Club (on the beachfront), ph 395 343 - open daily for lunch noon-2pm, Thurs-Tues for dinner 6-9pm.

Beaches Bistro, Rosslyn Bay Inn Resort, ph 336 300 - open daily 7am until late with live entertainment Wed to Sun, including Sunday lunch.

Pizza Pizzazz, Shop 4, 26 James Street, ph 394 422 - open Sat, Mon and Wed-Fri 10.30am-late; Tues 4.30pm-late; Sun

11am-late.

Footlights Restaurant and Theatre, 123 Old Rockhampton Road, ph 392 399 - fully licensed with great food and entertainment.

ENTERTAINMENT

Many of the resorts and hotels have live entertainment on various nights, so it is best to check with the information office to find out what's on where.

SIGHTSEEING

Cooberrie Park, 15km north of Yeppoon is a bird and animal sanctuary with barbecue and picnic facilities. If you want to pat a kangaroo, this is the place. They also have koalas and other native animals wandering freely through the parkland.

Byfield State Forest Parks are 17km north of Cooberrie Park, and are popular picnic areas. They include Stoney Creek, Waterpark Creek and Red Rock Forest Parks.

Nob Creek Pottery, established in 1979, is located in the Byfield Forest, and has gained a reputation as a quality cottage industry.

Wreck Point, at Cooee Bay, provides a spectacular view overlooking the Keppel group of islands. It is situated on the southern outskirts of Yeppoon.

Rosslyn Bay boat harbour is the base for a large fishing fleet, and the port for the many cruise and charter boats that service Great Keppel and the Islands. There are also accommodation facilities, restaurant, kiosk, fishermen's co-operative, boating supplies and coast guard information.

The 17km of *Scenic Highway* from Yeppoon south to Emu Park offer great views, safe beaches, and some very good fishing spots.

Emu Park has an unusual memorial to Captain Cook - a singing ship. The mast, sail and rigging contain hollow pipes, and the ship "sings" when the wind blows. The town has an hotel, restaurant, accommodation facilities, caravan park, arts and crafts shops, a historical museum and an information centre.

MACKAY

Mackay is surrounded by miles and miles of sugarcane fields, which give the city its title Sugar Capital of Australia.

North-east of Mackay, just off the coast from Shute Harbour, is the Whitsunday Group of Islands, containing some of the most popular of the resort islands of the Great Barrier Reef. Although these islands are not coral cays, the scenery is not so different from everyone's idea of a tropical paradise.

HOW TO GET THERE

By Air

Qantas Airlines has daily services to Mackay from Brisbane and Cairns.
Ansett Airlines has daily services to Mackay from Brisbane.
Flight West Airlines flies daily to Mackay from Brisbane and Cairns.

By Bus

McCafferty's Coaches and Greyhound/Pioneer have daily services to Mackay from Brisbane and Cairns.

By Rail

The *Sunlander* travels from Brisbane to Mackay on Tues, Thurs and Sat, and from Cairns on Mon, Thurs and Sat.

The *Queenslander* travels from Brisbane on Sun and Cairns on Tues.

The *Spirit of the Tropics* travels from Brisbane on Thursday and from Proserpine on Friday.

By Road

From Brisbane via the Bruce Highway, 976km. To drive to Shute Harbour, continue along the Bruce Highway to Proserpine (127km), then take the turn-off to Airlie Beach and Shute Harbour.

Mackay is 1079km south of Cairns.

TOURIST INFORMATION

Tourism Mackay Inc, "The Mill", 320 Nebo Road, Mackay, 4740, ph (079) 522 677; fax (079) 522 034. The office is open Mon-Fri 8.30am-5pm, Sat-Sun 9am-4pm. The building is a replica of the Richmond Sugar Mill, one of the earliest in the region. Apart from information the visitor centre also has souvenirs, a kiosk, a picnic area and ample parking.

ACCOMMODATION

Here is a selection of accommodation in Mackay and its environs, with prices for a double room per night, which should be used as a guide only. The telephone area code is 079.

Mackay

Ocean International, 1 Bridge Road, ph 572 044 - restaurant, swimming pool and spa, tennis court - $110.00.

Shakespeare International, 309 Shakespeare Street, ph 531 111 - restaurant, swimming pool and spa - $75.00.

Four Dice Motel, 166-170 Nebo Road, ph 511 555 - restaurant, swimming pool and spa - $75.00.

Marco Polo Motel, 46-50 Nebo Road, ph 512 700 - restaurant, swimming pool and spa, sauna - $73.

Lantern Motor Inn, 149-151 Nebo Road, ph 512 188 - restaurant, swimming pool and spa - $69.00.

White Lace Motor Inn, 73-75 Nebo Road, ph 514 466 - restaurant, swimming pool, some units suitable for disabled people - $69.00.

Alara Motor Inn, 52 Nebo Road, ph 512 699 - restaurant, swimming pool and spa, some units suitable for disabled people - $60.00.

Country Plaza Motor Inn, 40-42 Nebo Road, ph 576 526 - restaurant, swimming pool and spa - $52.00.

Riverside Holiday Units, 480 Bridge Road, ph 572 501 - cooking facilities, swimming pool and spa - $42.00.

Ocean Resort Village, 5 Bridge Road, ph 513 200 - cooking facilities, swimming pool, tennis courts - $65.00.

Metro Motor Inn, 34-38 Nebo Road, ph 511 811 - restaurant, swimming pool and spa, some units suitable for disabled people - $50.00.

Coral Sands Motel, 44 MacAlister Street, ph 511 244 - restaurant, swimming pool, some units suitable for disabled people - $50.00.

Paradise Lodge Motel, Peel Street, ph 513 644 - $46.00.

Golden Reef Motel, Nebo Road, ph 576 572 - restaurant, swimming pool - $40.00.

Rover Holiday Units, 174 Nebo Road, ph 513 711 - cooking facilities, swimming pool, some units suitable for disabled people - $38.00.

Cool Palms Motel, 4-6 Nebo Road, ph 575 477 - some units have cooking facilities, swimming pool - $38.00.

Bona Vista Motel, cnr Malcomson & Norris Streets, ph 422 211 - restaurant, swimming pool - $34.00.

Mia Mia Motel, 191 Nebo Road, ph 521 466 - swimming pool - $38.00.

Boomerang Motel/Hotel, Nebo Road, ph 521 755 - restaurant, swimming pool - $35.00.

Budget Accommodation

Kooyong Motor Hotel, Harbour Road, North Mackay, ph 514 844 - $37.00.

International Lodge, 40 MacAlister Street, ph 511 022 - $36.00.

Mackay Townhouse, 73 Victoria Street, ph 576 985 - $35.00.

Austral Hotel, 189 Victoria Street, ph 513 288 - $30.00.

Taylors Hotel, cnr Wood & Alfred Streets, ph 572 500 - $15.00.

Northern Beaches (approximately 15 minutes drive north of Mackay)

Kohuna Beach Resort, The Esplanade, Bucasia, ph 548 555 - restaurant, swimming pool and spa, some units suitable for disabled people, tennis court - $82.00+.

Dolphin Heads Resort, Beach Road, Dolphin Heads, ph 549 666 - restaurant, swimming pool and spa, some units suitable for disabled people, tennis court - $72.00+.

Pacific Palms Beachfront Units, Symons Avenue, Bucasia, ph 546 277 - cooking facilities, swimming pool, some units suitable for disabled people - $62.00+.

The Shores, 9 Pacific Drive, Blacks Beach, ph 548 322 - cooking facilities, swimming pool and spa, some units suitable for disabled people, tennis court - $50.00+.

Blue Pacific Village, 24 Bourke Street, Blacks Beach, ph 546 166 - cooking facilities, swimming pool - $42.00+.

Loafer Lodges Flats, 64 Waverley Street, Bucasia, ph 546 308 - cooking facilities, swimming pool - $35.00.

La Solana Units, Pacific Drive, Blacks Beach, ph 549 544 - cooking facilities, swimming pool, tennis court - $34.00+.

Hibiscus Coast (approximately 40-45 minutes drive north of Mackay)

Cape Hillsborough Resort, via Seaforth, ph 590 152 - restaurant, some units with cooking facilities, swimming pool - $60.00+.

Halliday Bay Resort, Halliday Bay, via Seaforth, ph 590 121 - restaurant, cooking facilities, swimming pool, tennis court - $52.00+.

Sarina (approximately 30 minutes drive south of Mackay)

Sandpiper Motel, Owen Jenkins Drive, Sarina, ph 566 130 - cooking facilities, tennis court - $45.00.

Hay Point Hotel/Motel, Hay Point, ph 563 266 - restaurant, some units with cooking facilities, swimming pool - $40.00.

Kinchant Dam (approximately 30 minutes drive west of Mackay)

Kinchant Waters Resort, Kinchant Dam, ph 541 453 - restaurant, cooking facilities, some units suitable for disabled people - camp site $8.00, Cabin $10.00 per person.

Eungella National Park (approximately 1 hours drive west of Mackay)

Broken River Mountain Retreat, Eungella, ph 584 528 - restaurant, cooking facilities in some units, swimming pool - $48.00+.

Eungella Chalet, Dalrymple Heights, Eungella, ph 584 509 - restaurant, cooking facilities in some units, swimming pool, tennis court, full board accommodation available - $35.00 room only.

Platypus Bush Camp, Finch Hatton Gorge Road, Finch Hatton, ph 583 204 - camp site $7.00, bush hut (1-4 people) $45.00.

Caravan Parks

Andergrove Van Park, Beaconsfield Road, North Mackay, ph 424 922 - swimming pool, camp kitchen, playground, shop, amenities for disabled people - powered sites $13.00; cabins with ensuite $36.00; on-site vans (with ensuite) $26.00.

Bucasia Beachfront Caravan Resort, The Esplanade, Bucasia, ph 546 375 - absolute beachfront, boat ramp adjacent - powered sites $14.00; cabins with ensuite $40.00.

Tropical Caravan Park, 185 Broadsound Road, ph 521 211 - swimming pool, games room, shop, facilities for disabled people - powered sites $14.00, cabins with ensuite $44.00-47.00.

Orange Grove Caravan Park, Mackay-Eungella Road, Marian, ph 543 301 - kiosk, near fishing and bushwalking, facilities for disabled people - powered sites $14.00; on-site vans $18.00.

Ocean Water Caravan Park, Condor Parade, Midge Point, ph 476 144 - swimming pool, playground, facilities for disabled people - powered sites $12.50; cabins with ensuite $40.00.

CAR HIRE

The following car rental companies have offices in Mackay -
Avis, Sydney Street, ph 511 266
Thrifty Rentals, Mangrove Road, ph 573 677
Budget Rentals, Sydney Street, ph 511 400
Hertz Rentals, Victoria Street, ph 572 662
Network Rentals, Victoria Street, ph 531 022
Cut Rate Rentals, Victoria Street, ph 531 616
Handy Car Rentals, Shell Service Station, City Gates, ph 521 372.

Loading Sugar Cane near Mackay

EATING OUT

Most of the motels have licensed restaurants, and many hotels serve inexpensive counter meals. Here is a listing of restaurants from which to choose.

Pippi's, Palmer Street, North Mackay, ph 511 376 - Italian Bistro.

Lychee Gardens, cnr Victoria & Wellington Streets, Mackay, ph 513 939 - Chinese.

The Beachouse, Ocean Avenue, Slade Point, ph 511 948 - Seafood.

Hogs Breath Cafe, Wood Street, Mackay, ph 577 799 - Bistro.

Alara Licensed Restaurant, 68 Victoria Street, Mackay, ph 512 699 - A la carte.

The Banquet House, 68 Victoria Street, Mackay, ph 511 003 - Chinese.

Crossroads Diner, 142 Nebo Road, Mackay, ph 572 468 - Licensed restaurant with Buffet dining.

White Lace Restaurant, 73 Nebo Road, Mackay, ph 514 466 - A la carte.

Supperhouse Garden, 136 Wood Street, Mackay, ph 577 266 - BYO cafe.

Coral Reef Restaurant, 40 Nebo Road, Mackay, ph 576 526 - A la carte.

Courtyard Carvery, 45 Wood Street, Mackay, ph 572 249.

The Creperie, 9 Gregory Street, Mackay, ph 511 226.

Classics Rock Cafe, cnr Sydney & Shakespeare Streets, Mackay, ph 535 035.

Rajput, Sydney Street, Mackay, 535 111 - Indian.

Mariner, 44 Victoria Street, Mackay, ph 573 279 - Seafood.

Shamrock Bar & Grill, 165 Nebo Road, Mackay, ph 572 629.

ENTERTAINMENT

If you fancy seeing a movie, head for Gordon Street and its five theatre complex. Or for some live entertainment contact the Mackay Entertainment Centre, also in Gordon Street, ph 572 255, and find out what the current offering is. The

Conservatorium of Music, 418 Shakespeare Street has regular classical and jazz concerts, often featuring overseas artists, and their number is 573 727.

Night owls have several nightclubs to tempt them:

The Blue Moose, 1st floor, The Dome, Victoria Street (entry through Wilkies Hotel), ph 577 737.

The Balcony, Wilkinsons Hotel, cnr Gregory & Victoria Streets, ph 572 241.

Generator's Nite Club, 10 Carlyle Street, ph 531 988.

Paro's Night Club, 85 Victoria Street, ph 514 365.

Huckleberries, 99 Victoria Street, ph 573 965.

Mermaid Club, Ocean International, 1 Bridge Road, ph 572 044.

Manhattans on the Terrace, The Ambassador Hotel, Sydney Street, ph 572 368.

Jimmy Dean's, Prince of Wales Hotel, River Street, ph 514 933 (Wed & Fri).

The Loaded Dog, Australian Hotel, cnr Wood & Victoria Streets, ph 572 220.

If you are in town on a *Thursday* night you might like to go to the greyhound racing at the Mackay Showground in Milton Street. If it is a *Saturday* night when you are looking for something to do, trip off to the Glenella Hall and the Mackay Ballroom Dancers' Club. The dance program is 50% Old-time, 40% New Vogue and 10% Modern, and for more information phone Ivy on 423 636 or Daphne on 554 001.

SHOPPING

Centrepoint Shopping Centre, ph 572 229, is in Victoria Street, in the heart of the city, where you will also find some good street shopping.

Caneland Shoppingtown, ph 513 311, is in Mangrove Road, and behind it is the Caneland Park Music Shell were the annual Sugartime Festival, among other entertainment, is held.

Mt Pleasant Shopping Centre, Phillip Street, North Mackay, ph 421 069, is more convenient for those staying to the north of the city.

Weekend markets are held as follows:

Mackay Walkers Bazaar on Harbour Road - Sat-Sun 8am-4pm.

Mackay Showground Markets - Sat 8am-noon.
Seaforth Markets - Sun 9am-2pm.
 On the first Sunday of every month the Bucasia Craft Markets are held at the Bucasia Community Hall 9am-1pm, and on most long weekends the Eungella Markets are staged at Dalrymple Heights Oval.

Arts & Crafts

Mackay Art and Craft Gallery, 308 Shakespeare Street, ph 576 977, is open Wed-Sun 10am-4pm, or by appointment Mon and Tues. Stocks paintings, pottery and all kinds of arts and crafts.
Mackay Art Centre, 133 Victoria Street, ph 574 200, has a gallery of locally made pottery, blown glass, floral sculpture, woodwork, jewellery and handmade paper. It is open Mon-Fri 9am-5pm, Sat 9am-noon.
Forbes Gallery, 68 George Street, ph 576 837, is the workshops of established pastel and acrylic artist Clem Forbes. It is open daily 10am-6pm.
Pioneer Potters in Swayne Street, North Mackay, ph 576 255, has a good selection of handmade local pottery and sculpture. It is open Wed and Sat 10am-4pm.
The Fisherman's Glass, 5 Andergrove Road, North Mackay, ph 553 421, features the work of glass craftsman John Anthony. His hand-blown fish, corals, shells and "Reef Window" paperweights are very popular with visitors to this part of the world. Open Mon-Fri 9am-3pm and most Sun afternoons.
The Beach Pottery, 6 Blacks Beach Road, Blacks Beach, ph 549 667, offers functional stoneware pottery by local potters. It is open Mon-Thurs 10am-5pm, and weekends by arrangement.
Bucasia Gardens and Gifts, on the Mackay-Bucasia Road about ten minutes drive past Mt Pleasant Shopping Centre, has a wide selection of local pottery, crafts, dried flowers and giftware. It is open daily 9.30am-5pm, ph 548 134, and also has a coffee shop, plants and pots.
Homebush Store Pottery & Craft Gallery is situated 26km south-west of Mackay in an historic building. Opening in the early 1900 as the local store for the people of Homebush and

surrounding areas, it has now been restored and is operated as a pottery workshop. Also available are works of art, fibre arts, woodturned objects, hand painted T-shirts and handmade cane baskets. The Gallery is open Fri-Tues 9am-5pm, ph 597 339.

Bente Christensen's North Eton Pottery Store Gallery, Marian Road, North Eton (about 30km south-west of Mackay), ph 541 232, is open Thurs-Mon 9.30am-5.30pm. It has stocks of pottery, paintings, arts and crafts.

SIGHTSEEING

John Mackay discovered the Pioneer River Valley in 1860, but he named the river the Mackay. He returned with stock and registered "Greenmount" the first pastoral run in the district in 1862. Others followed and the settlement was named Mackay in his honour. The river's name, however, had to be changed to Pioneer because there was already a Mackay River.

It was only a few years before sugar became the main industry, pioneered by the efforts of John Spiller, T. Henry FitzGerald and John Ewen Davidson. Nowadays Mackay Harbour is home to the world's largest bulk sugar terminal.

The tourist information centre can provide maps and information for: a one-and-a-half hour Heritage Walk through the city visiting all the historic old buildings; and for a half-day Heritage Drive through the valley to the former gold rush settlement of Eungella, passing through the towns of Walkerston, Marian, Mirani, Gargett, Pinnacle and Finch Hatton.

The port for Mackay was originally on the river, but because of the enormous tides (around 6.5m), a new port was built on the coast.

Queen's Park Orchid House, cnr Gordon & Goldsmith Streets, has an excellent display of native and foreign orchids. The park is open Mon-Fri 10.30am-11am, 2-2.30pm and Sun 2-5pm.

Illawong Fauna Sanctuary, at Illawong Beach, 4km from Mackay centre, is a beachfront recreation area amid tropical landscaping. There are kangaroos roaming free, a pool, trampoline, video games and full catering facilities, as well as crocodiles (not roaming free). The sanctuary is open daily with feeding times at 9am, 11.30am and 3.30pm, and admission is $2.00. For further information ph 577 591.

You can get a good panoramic view of the city and the countryside from the *Mt Oscar Lookout* in Norris Road, North Mackay.

Tours of *Farleigh Mill* are conducted Mon-Fri at 1.00pm during the crushing season, from June to November. A trained, local hostess will take you on a 2-hour tour, afternoon tea is included, and is all costs $10.00 adults, $5.00 children. Bookings can be made through SkillShare, ph 574 727 or the tourist information centre.

Beaches

Illawong (Far Beach) and *Iluka* (Town Beach) offer views of Flat and Round Top Islands and Dalrymple Bay/Hay Point coal loading terminal.

Harbour Beach has a surf lifesaving patrol, toilets, adventure playground and picnic area.

Lamberts Beach has a lookout that provides island views.

Blacks Beach is a long secluded beach with picnic facilities.

Dolphin Heads has accommodation available.

Eimeo Beach has a small picnic area next to an avenue of century old mango trees.

Sunset Beach has a shaded foreshore picnic area.

Bucasia Beach has a summer swimming enclosure, picnic area and views to Dolphin Heads and islands.

Shoal Point Beach has a picnic area, toilets and lookout. The esplanade offers views of islands, Cape Hillsborough and Hibiscus Coast, and there is a causeway to Little Green Island.

SOUTH OF MACKAY

Twenty-five kilometres south of Mackay is the *Hay Point & Dalrymple Bay Coal Terminal Complex*, the largest coal export facility in the southern hemisphere. The wharves stretch 3.8km out to sea, and coal trains up to 2km long arrive at the port daily. The Port Administration Building has recorded information and a viewing platform.

The *Big Prawn* is at lot 1, Grasstree Beach Road, Grasstree Beach, and is the only commercial hatchery in Australia that is open to the public.

The sugar town of *Sarina* is 37km south of Mackay. It has a population of around 3,500, some picturesque scenery, and some excellent beaches.

Cape Palmerston National Park is 80km south of Mackay and has 4WD only access. It offers long sandy beaches, palm forests, freshwater lagoons and large stands of melaleuca. Attractions include **Ince Bay** to the north, **Temple Island** and the volcanic plug of **Mt Funnel**. There is camping, but facilities are very basic.

Beaches

Campwin Beach, 8.5km from Sarina, is home to a rich fishing and prawning industry. Boat launching and mooring facilities are available and there is easy access to nearby islands.

Armstrong Beach is 9.5km from Sarina and has a picnic and camping, and an orchid nursery that is open by appointment only.

Sarina Beach, 13km from Sarina, has a picnic area, store, boat ramp, and a surf lifesaving patrol. Coral Lookout is at the southern end of the beach.

Grasstree Beach, 13km from Sarina, has a picnic area and boat ramp in a wide sheltered bay.

Salonika Beach, 24km from Sarina, is a quiet sandy beach with an inland lagoon teeming with birdlife.

Halftide Beach, 28km from Sarina, is home to the Tug Boat Harbour that services Hay Point Coal Terminal.

NORTH OF MACKAY

Cape Hillsborough National Park, 45km north-east of Mackay, covers 830ha and features a variety of vegetation, elevated lookouts and peaceful beaches. The staff of the Cape Hillsborough Resort hand feed the various native animals, so it is not unusual to see a couple of kangaroos lazing on the beach undisturbed by humans doing the same thing.

Cathu State Forest is 70km north of Mackay. Drive along the Bruce Highway to 3km north of Yalboroo, turn left and continue for 12km along the gravel road to the Forestry Office. Within the forest is the Jaxut State Forest Park which has shaded picnic areas with friendly kangaroos, camping facilities and toilets. To find out about other attractions in the forest, especially the swimming hole and the Clarke Ranges lookout, contact the Ranger on 475 736.

Midge Point is reached by turning right of the Bruce Highway at Bloomsbury, and travelling 18km through the Condor Hill to the village of Midgetown. Named after a small survey vessel, the *Midge*, in the early 1920s, this area has been 'discovered' by developers, and has become a tourist destination.

Nearby *Laguna Quays Resort* has 4km of ocean frontage and a championship standard golf course, and its accommodation gives the choice of waterfront or golf course views. There is also a 60 room Golf Lodge, a Racquet Club, and of course, a swimming pool.

NOTES

Beaches

Roughly 25km north of Mackay, turn right onto Seaforth Road then travel 20km to the *Hibiscus Coast*. This includes the beachside settlements of Seaforth, Halliday Bay, Ball Bay and Cape Hillsborough. These beaches are all nesting sites for green and flatback turtles who lay their eggs during the three month period from October each year. The baby turtles hatch between late January and early April.

Halliday Bay has a sandy beach swimming enclosure, accommodation and a restaurant. It is reached from Cape Hillsborough Road.

Seaforth is 48km north-east of Mackay, and offers camping and picnic facilities overlooking the beach.

Belmunda Bay is reached by turning right about 5km along the Cape Hillsborough Road. The bay has secluded beaches with several fishing shacks. After rain has fallen, the nearby freshwater lakes are visited by crowds of water birds, including the brolga.

SPORT

Golf

There are three golf courses within 40km of Mackay city:

Mackay Golf Club, Northern Beaches Road, Mackay.

The Valley Golf Club, Leichhardt Street, Mirani.

Sarina Golf Club, Golf Links Road, Sarina.

Swimming

The *Memorial Swimming Pool*, Milton Street, ph 516 533, is near Caneland Shopping Centre. It is open Tues, Thurs and Fri 5am-8.45pm, Wed, Sat and Sun 5am-6pm (closed June and early July) and admission is $1.

The *Pioneer Swim Centre*, Malcomson Street, North Mackay, has an olympic swimming pool, a picnic area and an adventure playground. It is open Mon, Wed and Thurs 6am-8pm, Tues, Fri-Sun 6am-6pm (closed May 31 to August 1), ph 575 767.

Whitsunday Waterworld, Harbour Road, Mackay, ph 553 851, is a complex with waterslides, mini golf, pinball, video machines and kiosk. It is open Sat-Sun and school holidays 10am-10pm.

Indoor Sports

BG's Sports Centre on the Bruce Highway south of the City Gates, is one of the largest indoor recreational and fitness centres in Australia. It offers tenpin bowling, roller skating, squash and many other sports, ph 521 509. It is open daily 9am-midnight.

Fishing Charters

Whyllaway Cruises, ph 511 555 - $1500 per day charter hire, all inclusive.

Eagle Fishing Day Tours, ph 421 883 - fishing the Pioneer River Estuary - $50 per person, including tackle, bait and lunch.

Elizabeth E. Cruises (Great Barrier Reef), ph 574 281 - Thurs-Sun $150 per person (min 20 people).

Gordies Mackay Beaches Fishing Tours, ph 546 898 - half day trips 7am-noon, 1.30-6pm - $35 per person, including 'smoko', bait and gear.

Pioneer Boat Hire, ph 546 605 - 6Hp $35 per day - no boat licence required.

Mackay Sports Fishing Safaris, ph 576 014 - 4.6m customised boat in local rivers, creeks and dams, with equipment provided - 7 days a week, $250 per boat for a full day.

Waiben Cruises, ph 574 317 - cruise the Whitsundays for snorkelling, fishing and reef exploring.

Diving

Mackay Adventure Divers, ph 511 472 - reef trip and dive, Mon, Wed & Fri $130 per person. Snorkelling safaris including lesson and tour of Credlin Reef - $15 per person including gear.

TOURS

Bush Safari to Eungella and Finch Hatton - daily - $50 adult, $25 child (5-16), ph 531 000.

Cape Hillsborough National Park Tour - Fridays and *Hay Point/Sarine Tour* - Saturdays - $45 adults, $27 child under 14, ph 562 287.

Brigitte's Tropical Tours, ph 015 632 521, has Sunset Tours and day tours to Cape Hillsborough and Eungella.

Transfer to Cape Hillsborough (Resort Coach) Mon-Fri - $20 return, weekends by arrangement, ph 590 152.

CRUISES

The Great Barrier Reef can be reached from Mackay by sea and air. Credlin Reef, one of the 2100 reefs that make up this coral colony, is only 2 to 3 hours from Mackay Harbour by high speed catamaran. There is a shaded pontoon, underwater viewing area and a seasub that make for excellent snorkelling, scuba diving and coral viewing.

Bushy Atoll, a half-hour seaplane flight from Mackay airport, is the only quay on the entire Reef to have an enclosed lagoon.

Roylen Cruises, Harbour Road, ph 553 066, have the following on offer, all departing from Mackay Harbour.

Brampton Island - daily - departs Mackay at 9am, returns at 4.50pm on Sun, Tues, Thurs and Sat, 5.45pm on Mon, Wed and Fri - cost, including lunch, is $45.

Lindeman Island - Sun, Tues, Thurs and Sat - departs Mackay at 9am, returns at 4.50pm - cost, including lunch, is $90.

Hamilton Island - Sun, Tues, Thurs and Sat - departs Mackay at 9am, returns at 4.50pm - cost is $40.

Great Barrier Reef - Mon, Wed and Fri - departs Mackay at 9am, returns at 5.45pm - cost, including lunch and coral viewing, is $95.00.

Elizabeth E II Coral Cruises, 102 Goldsmith Street, Mackay, ph (079) 574 281, fax (079) 572 268, offer trips from two to 21 days aboard their specially built monohull dive and fishing boat, zabeth E II. The boat is stabilised and has the latest navigation aids, as well as 240v throughout and a 110v charging system.

Accommodation for 12 to 28 passengers are in one double, 12

twin and two triple berths with en-suite facilities and unlimited fresh water. All meals are chef-prepared and snacks, weights, air and tanks are included in the charter costs.

SCENIC FLIGHTS

Helijet, Mackay Airport, ph (079) 577 400; Hamilton Island Airport, ph (079) 468249; Cairns Airport, ph (070) 359 300, offer (prices are per person):

Helicopter Reef Discovery Flight - 2 hours - $325.

Helicopter Fly-Cruise Reef Trip 4 1/2 hours - $245. Standby return $170.

Helicopter Adventure Flight - 15 minutes - $99.

Helicopter Reef Joyflight - 10 minutes - $65.

Helicopter Champagne Flight - 2 1/2 hours - $290; with cold meat/salad luncheon $325; with seafood/salad luncheon $335.

Seaplane Reefcomber Flight - 3 hours - $255.

Seaplane Whitehaven Fun Seeker - 2 hours - $155.

Flights of Fantasy - 15 minutes - $65.

                      - 30 minutes - $89.

                      - 60 minutes - $135.

Tiger Moth   - 20 minutes - $99.

                      - 40 minutes - $190.

Helijet also have fixed wing flights between Hamilton Island, Lindeman Island and Mackay, and the costs are:

Hamilton Island/Lindeman Island - $45.

Hamilton Island/Mackay - $95.

Lindeman Island/Mackay - $80.

Fredericksons, ph 423 161 have daily/tidal flights by seaplane to Bushy Atoll, with a landing, for around $160 per person.

Air Pioneer, ph 576 661, offer the above for around the same price, as well as charter flights.

Osprey Island Air Tours, ph 422 987, offer a two hour flight over the Whitsundays with a three hour stopover on either Brampton or Hamilton Islands. Contact them for further information.

WHITSUNDAY ISLANDS

The Whitsundays consist of 74 islands from the Cumberland and Northumberland Island groups, and they form the largest offshore island chain on Australia's east coast.

The islands are the remains of a mountain range that was drowned when sea levels rose at the end of the last ice age. Most of them have National Park status, and all are situated in a marine park. There are basic camping facilities on Hook, North Molle, Whitsunday, Henning, Border, Haslewood, Shaw, Thomas and Repulse Islands. These consist of toilets and picnic tables, with a ranger patrolling. Costs are $2/person/night ($10/site/night for family group with no more than 2 persons over 15 years). Camping permits must be obtained from QNP&WS, and their closest office is at Airlie Beach.

The islands were named by, you've guessed it, Captain Cook when he sailed through the passage on Whitsunday, 1770. Actually, there are those who like to point out that it was not actually Whitsunday because the good old captain had not taken into account the fact that he had crossed the international date line and so was a day out. I think we should let him get away with this small error, as he didn't make too many.

When European settlement began on several of the islands there were some violent confrontations with the resident Aborigines.

CLIMATE

This is a tropical, sub-rainforest region. Daytime temperatures April-October are 20 to 24C, night are 14 to 18C. During November-March, the "green season", daytime are 24 to 30C, and night are 18 to 26C. The water temperature remains 20 to 22C throughout the year.

BRAMPTON ISLAND

Brampton is part of the Cumberland Group of Islands and is about 32km north-east of Mackay at the entrance to the Whitsunday Passage. The island is a National Park, with an area of 4.6 sq km. It is connected to Carlisle Island and to Pelican Island by sand bars that can be crossed at low tide.

A mountainous island with lush forests, nature trails, kangaroos and emus, Brampton also has seven sandy beaches and is surrounded by coral reefs. The walk around the island is about 7km, takes around three hours, and is best done in a clockwise direction. There is a walk up to the island's highest point, Brampton Peak, beginning near the resort golf course and the round trip takes about two hours. Both walks offer great views.

Although, obviously, Captain Cook was in the area he either didn't see Brampton or he wasn't interested, because the island was not named and surveyed until 1879.

In the early 1900s the Queensland government used the island as a nursery for palm trees, which accounts for the abundance of those trees now.

The Busuttin family moved to Brampton in 1916 to breed chinchilla rabbits, and when this proved unsuccessful they tried their hand at raising goats and horses for the British Army in India. In 1933 the family opened a resort, but they kept the livestock side going until just after the war, when they needed more space for visitors. The Busuttins sold the resort in 1959, and it went through several pairs of hands before becoming the property of the Roylen group, who still handle the boat transfers from Mackay to Brampton. In 1985 Australian Airlines took over the resort, and then later they themselves were taken over by Qantas, the present owners, who have made many alterations and additions.

Sunrise over the Whitsunday Passage

HOW TO GET THERE

By Air

Qantas has three flights daily to Brampton Island from Mackay, and the trip takes 20 minutes.

By Sea

Roylen Cruises, ph 553 066, depart Mackay at 9am and the return fare is $45.

There is a mini-railway that transports visitors from the wharf to the resort.

ACCOMMODATION

Brampton Island Resort has two style of accommodation - 26 Blue Lagoon Beachfront units and 66 Blue Lagoon Garden Units.

Resort facilities are: restaurant, cocktail bar, two swimming pools, spa, games room, tennis courts, cafe, kids' club, surf skis, gymnasium, tube rides, golf, waterskiing, catamaran sailing, sailboarding, beach volleyball, snorkelling, cruising and coral viewing, Barrier Reef trips, EFTPOS.

Room facilities are: balcony or verandah, tea and coffee making facilities, refrigerator, colour TV, in-house movies, IDD/STD telephone, radio, air-conditioning, daily cleaning service.

Tariffs for one night per person/twin share are:

Garden - $122 adult (child 3-14 years sharing with 2 adults - free)

Beachfront - $136 adult (child - as above)

Maximum occupancy of both style units: 4 persons (child is counted as a person).

The above rates are room only, but there is a meal option, with costs for one night as follows:

Breakfast - $18 adult, $9 child

Breakfast and Dinner - $47.00 adult, $24 child

Full Board - $65 adult, $33 child.

Additional to the tariff are: Great Barrier Reef Cruises, Great Barrier Reef Flights, Bullet Rides, Fishing Trips, Forest Walk (day), Melaleuca Tour on Carlisle Island, Scuba Diving Lessons and Trips, Water Skiing, Whitsunday Island Cruises.

Reservations can be made through Australian Resorts, ph 008 812 525 (7 days), from overseas ph (+ 61 7) 360 2444, or through any Qantas office. The Resort address is Brampton Island Resort, Brampton Island, Qld, 4740, ph (079) 514 499, fax (079) 514 097.

Credit cards accepted: Visa, MasterCard, Bankcard, Diners Club, American Express, JCB.

EATING OUT

The *Carlisle Restaurant* is the main dining room where people on the meal plan usually dine. If you are paying separately for your food there is the *Saltwater Rocks Bar & Cafe* which is open for lunch and dinner and serves sandwiches, salads and light meals. This is where the day trippers usually stop for a bite to eat.

DIVING

There is nothing at Brampton itself to excite divers, but cruises from Mackay to Credlin Reef aboard the *Spirit of Roylen*, ph (079) 553 066, call in at Brampton to pick up and put down. Credlin Reef is in the Hydrographers Passage area, and there is a permanent pontoon over the reef, an underwater observatory and a semi-submersible. Resort diving courses are conducted on board the *Spirit of Roylen* in transit to Credlin Reef, or at the Resort by special arrangements.

AIRLIE BEACH

The town of Airlie Beach borders the 24,000ha Conway National Park, and is the mainland centre for the Whitsundays.

Airlie Beach is a picturesque village and offers a lot to the holidaymaker on its own account, but when you add the close proximity of the Reef islands, it is not hard to figure out why some people chose to stay at Airlie and day trip to the islands.

HOW TO GET THERE

By Air

Ansett Australia, *Qantas* and *Sunstate* have daily flights from Brisbane to Proserpine, and it is a short drive from there to Airlie Beach.

By Rail

The *Sunlander* departs Brisbane for Proserpine every Tues, Thurs and Sat. The return journey departs Cairns every Mon, Thurs and Sat.

By Bus

Pioneer/Greyhound and McCafferty's stop at Proserpine on their Brisbane-Cairns trips.

By Road

Proserpine is 127km north of Mackay, on the Bruce Highway.

TOURIST INFORMATION

Airlie Beach Information Office is on Shute Harbour Road, and the phone number is (079) 466 665.

ACCOMMODATION

Following is a selection of accommodation with prices for a double room per night, which should be used as a guide only. The telephone area code is 079.

Laguna Quays Resort, Kunapipi Springs Road, Repulse Bay, ph 477 777 - 20 minutes south of Proserpine airport - luxury accommodation with championship golf course, racquet club with pool, and all non-motorised activities included in tariff - $158+.

Club Crocodile Resort, Shute Harbour Road, Airlie Beach, ph 467 155 - restaurant, swimming pool and spa, tennis court, scuba diving - $99.

Coral Sea Resort, 25 Ocean View Avenue, Airlie Beach, ph 466 458 - restaurant, cocktail bar, swimming pool, tea/coffee making facilities - $99.

Coral Point Lodge, Harbour Avenue, Shute Harbour, ph 469 500 - restaurant, coffee shop, kitchen facilities, free transfers to Shute Harbour Jetty - $88.

Coral Point Lodge Retreat, Shute Harbour Road, Shute Harbour, ph 469 500 - cooking facilities, swimming pool - $75.

Paradise Court Units, 181 Shute Harbour Road, Airlie Beach, ph 467 139 - cooking facilities, swimming pool - $45+.

Island Gateway Caravan Village, Shute Harbour Road, Airlie Beach, ph 466 228 - swimming pool - tent site $12.00; powered sites $14.00; cabins $35.00; on-site vans $25-45.

Airlie Cove Resort Van Park, cnr Ferntree & Shute Harbour Roads, Jubilee Pocket, ph 466 727 - tent sites $12.00; powered sites $14.00; cabins from $30.00.

CRUISES

Fantasea Cruises, PO Box 616, Airlie Beach, 4802 ph (079) 465 111, fax (079) 465 520 offer:

Great Barrier Reef Day Cruise to Reefworld - semi-sub coral viewing, snorkelling equipment including hygienic mouthpiece, buffet lunch, morning and afternoon teas, fresh water showers and large sundeck area, courtesy pick-up from accommodation, large underwater viewing chamber - $108 adult, $53 child (4-14), $222 family - daily - 8.30am-5pm from Shute Harbour.

Three Island Adventure - visit Whitehaven Beach, Hamilton and Daydream Islands - beach games at Whitehaven and pool facilities at Daydream, morning and afternoon tea, courtesy pick-up - $55 adult, $27.50 child (4-14), $137.50 family - Mon,

Wed Fri, Sat, Sun - from Abel Point Marina - 9am-5pm.

Reef Adventure - spend approximately 3 1/2 hours at Reefworld, Fantasea's floating platform on the outer Great Barrier Reef - includes snorkelling, coral viewing in the semi-submersible, observing marine life in the underwater theatre, and a buffet lunch - $106 adult, $53 child (4-14), $222 family - daily - from Shute Harbour - 8.30am.

Whale Watching Day Cruise - these are usually held July-September, depending upon the arrival and departure of these fascinating creatures - $67 adult, $35 child, $169 family.

Hamilton Island Day Cruise - $35 adult, $17.50 child, $87.50 family - daily - from Shute Harbour - 8.30am.

Whitehaven Beach & Hamilton Island - $39 adult, $19.50 child, $97.50 family - Tues, Thurs, Sun - Shute Harbour - 8.30am.

Daydream Island Day Cruise - $67 adult, $35 child, $169 family - Mon, Wed, Fri, Sat, Sun - from Abel Point Marine - 9am.

Seatrek Whitsunday Cruises, PO Box 20, Airlie Beach, 4802, ph (079) 465 255, fax (079) 465 238, offer:

Three Island and Underwater Adventure Cruise - submarine ride at Hook Island, admission to underwater observatory at Hook Island, snorkelling (tide permitting), bbq lunch at Hook Island, visit Daydream Island, golf and bird feeding at South Molle Island - $49 adult, $24.50 child, $127 family - departs Shute Harbour - 9am.

Night Cruise to South Molle Island - includes poolside seafood smorgasbord, Polynesian floorshow, courtesy coach - Fri - $50 adult, $25 child - departs Shute Harbour - 6.30pm.

South Molle Island Day Trip - includes windsurfing, catamarans, paddle skis, golf - daily $25 adult, $12.50 child (half day trip $15 adult, $7.50 child) - departs Shute Harbour - 9am-5pm.

Whitsunday All Over Cruises, Shute Harbour Road (next to Airlie Hotel, Airlie Beach, 4802, ph (079) 466 900, fax (079) 465 763, incorporate *Whitsunday Water Taxis* and offer:

Daydream Island - $22 adult, $12 child, $56 family - daily - departs Shute Harbour 9am - returns 4.45pm.

Whitsunday Long Island - $22 adult, $12 child, $56 family - daily - departs Shute Harbour 9.15am - returns 4.30pm.

WHITSUNDAY GROUP

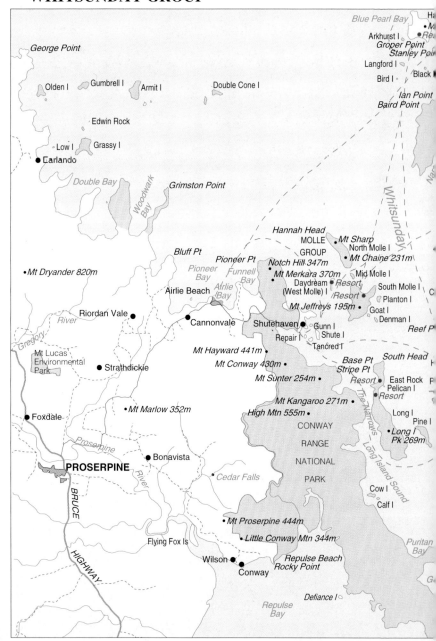

Blue Pearl Bay
Ha
M
Re
Arkhurst I
Groper Point
Stanley Poir
Langford I
Bird I
Black
Ian Point
Baird Point
George Point
Olden I
Gumbrell I
Armit I
Double Cone I
Edwin Rock
Low I
Grassy I
Earlando
Double Bay
Woodwark Bay
Grimston Point
Whitsunday
Nal
Hannah Head
MOLLE
GROUP
Mt Sharp
North Molle I
Mt Chaine 231m
Bluff Pt
Pioneer Pt
Notch Hill 347m
Pioneer Bay
Funnell Bay
Mt Merkara 370m
Mid Molle I
Daydream
Resort
South Molle I
Airlie Beach
Airlie Bay
Daydream (West Molle) I
Resort
Planton I
Mt Jeffreys 195m
Goat I
Riordan Vale
Cannonvale
Shutehaven
Gunn I
Denman I
Reef P
River
Gregory
Repair I
Shute I
Tancred I
Mt Hayward 441m
Mt Lucas Environmental Park
Strathdickie
Mt Conway 430m
Base Pt
South Head
Mt Sunter 254m
Stripe Pt
Resort
East Rock
Pelican I
Resort
Mt Kangaroo 271m
Foxdale
Mt Marlow 352m
High Mtn 555m
Long I
Pine I
CONWAY
Long I Pk 269m
Bonavista
RANGE
Proserpine River
PROSERPINE
NATIONAL
Cedar Falls
PARK
The Narrows
Long Island Sound
Cow I
Calf I
BRUCE
Mt Proserpine 444m
Puritan Bay
Flying Fox Is
Little Conway Mtn 344m
Wilson
Repulse Beach
Rocky Point
G
Conway
HIGHWAY
Defiance I
Repulse Bay

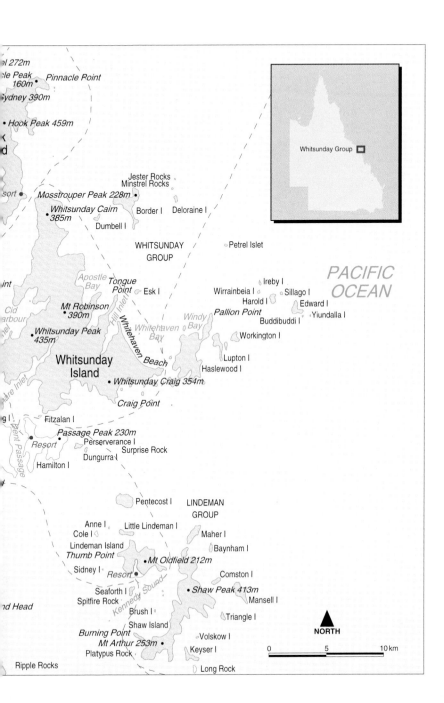

el 272m
cle Peak · Pinnacle Point
160m
ydney 390m

· Hook Peak 459m

K
d

sort · *Mosstrouper Peak 228m* ·

Jester Rocks
Minstrel Rocks

Whitsunday Cairn
385m · Border I   Deloraine I

Dumbell I

WHITSUNDAY
GROUP   ◦ Petrel Islet

int

Apostle Tongue
Bay Point ◦ Esk I

                                          ◦ Ireby I

PACIFIC
OCEAN

Wirrainbeia I ◦ ◦ Sillago I
Harold I ◦   ◦ Edward I
Pallion Point ◦ Yiundalla I
Buddibuddi I ◦

Cid
arbour

Mt Robinson
· 390m

Whitsunday Peak
435m

Windy
Bay

Whitehaven
Bay

Whitsunday
Island

Whitehaven Beach

Workington I

Lupton I
Haslewood I

· *Whitsunday Craig 354m*

Craig Point ·

g I ˎ
Resort ·

Fitzalan I

Passage Peak 230m
Persererverance I
Surprise Rock
Dungurra I

Hamilton I

◦ Pentecost I   LINDEMAN
GROUP

Anne I ◦ Little Lindeman I
Cole I ◦   Maher I
Lindeman Island
Thumb Point   ◦ Baynham I
Sidney I ◦ *Resort* · · *Mt Oldfield 212m*

◦ Comston I

Seaforth I ◦
Spitfire Rock   · *Shaw Peak 413m*
Brush I ◦   Mansell I

Shaw Island   ◦ Triangle I

Burning Point
Mt Arthur 253m ·
Platypus Rock   ◦ Volskow I
Keyser I

nd Head

Ripple Rocks

◦ Long Rock

NORTH

0   5   10 km

Palm Bay - $22 adult, $12 child, $56 family - daily - departs Shute Harbour 9.15am - returns 4.15pm.

South Molle Island - $25 adult, $13 child, $63 family - daily - departs Shute Harbour 9am - returns 5pm.

Club Med - Lindeman Island - $100 adult, $51 child - daily - departure times available the day prior to departure.

Daydream Island Evening - $22 adult, $12 child - nightly - departs Shute Harbour 5.15pm - returns 11.15pm. Meals are extra and are as follows: Monday - Italian - $24.50.

Tuesday - English Carvery - $24.50.

Wednesday - Aussie BBQ - $26.50.

Thursday - French - $24.50.

Friday - Mexican - $24.50.

Saturday - Seafood - $35.50.

Sunday - International - $24.50.

Each evening's entertainment is different, but all promise a good time.

Yellow Sub Cruise - includes courtesy coach, morning tea, picnic lunch, snorkelling gear, talk by marine biologist, guided island tours, guided coral viewing in an air-conditioned semi-submersible, visit to Daydream Island Beach Club for approximately an hour before returning to the mainland - $58 adult, $29 child - $145 family - Tues-Sun - departs Shute Harbour at 9am, Daydream Island at 9.15am, South Molle at 9.30am - returns 5pm.

DIVING

Pro Dive - Whitsunday, PO Box 517, Airlie Beach, 4802, ph (079) 466508, fax (079) 465 007, is a PADI 5-Star dive centre. It has its own custom built diver training facility, with a 5m pool for the beginner or intermediate diver. Courses taught include entry level Openwater certification through to Instructor. Dive courses commence four times a week and comprise two days in the pool and class room plus three days and three nights practical lessons on a fully catered live-aboard reef cruise. The company has two live-aboard specialist dive/sail vessels, and take people to a variety of Barrier Reef dive sails.

Barrier Reef Diving Services, The Esplanade, Airlie Beach, 4802,

(opposite) A jetty in Shute Harbour.

ph (079) 466 204, fax (079) 465 130, is another PADI 5-Star training facility. They offer daily dive and snorkel trips to some of the best locations amongst the Whitsunday Islands, and the Barrier Reef. BRDS also has its own pool and classroom with modern teaching aids, and offers training from Openwater to Instructor on either a full-time or part-time basis. The dive shop is well stocked with equipment and accessories.

LINDEMAN ISLAND

Lindeman has an area of 8 sq km, most of which is national park, and was named after George Lindeman, whose job in the Royal Navy was to chart safe passages through the Whitsunday Islands.

The first resort was opened by Angus and Elizabeth Nicholson in 1923, and it stayed in their family until it was sold in 1979. Thora Nicholson, who was married to Angus and Elizabeth's son Loch, still lives on the island, in a timber house behind the new resort.

Lindeman has six beaches and 20km of walking trails. It's highest point is Mt Oldfield, 210m. There is a resident Park Ranger who will advise and even accompany walkers.

HOW TO GET THERE

See the *Flights* section in the Mackay chapter for Helijet services to the island, and see above *Cruise* section for boat trips from Shute Harbour.

Ansett Australia fly to Hamilton Island, and there is a 30 minute launch transfer to Lindeman.

ACCOMMODATION

Club Med opened its doors on Lindeman Island in 1992, and by 1994 had won the Hotel/Resort of the Year award.

Resort facilities are: boutique, restaurants, laundry, sports clubhouse, medical facilities, nightclub, recorded classical music concerts, card room, picnics, golf course (9-holes), tennis, aerobics, volleyball, basketball, archery, table tennis, football, cricket, badminton, hiking in the National Park, sailing, windsurfing, paddle skis, snorkelling, 2 swimming pools, seaboat trips, beach towels, Kids' Club.

Room facilities are: air-conditioning private bathroom, balcony/patio, TV, phone, bar fridge, tea/coffee making facilities, overhead ceiling fan.

Tariffs for one night per person/twin share are:

$195-250 adult, $95-125 child 4-11; $60-125 child 2-3; $20-25 child 0-1. The price ranges are for the lowest and the highest seasons. Transfer from Hamilton Island, one way, is $39 adult, $20 child.

The above rates include all meals plus meal time drinks (beer, wine and juices).

Club Med Holiday Packages include return economy air fares, transfers and insurance, and are really the only way to go. Here are some examples:

From Sydney - 5 days/4 nights - Jan-April - $1325 adult, $1235 child 12-14, $875 child 4-11.

From Brisbane - 5 days/4 nights - Jan-April - $1150 adult, $1105 child 12-14, $745 child 4-11.

From Melbourne - 5 days/4 nights - Jan-April - $1395 adult, $1310 child 12-14, $950 child 4-11.

Not included in the tariff are: the scuba diving course on the Great Barrier Reef, special excursions, and drinks at the bar.

Reservations can be made through any state Club Med Office, or direct through the Resort - Club Med, Lindeman Island, via Mackay, 4741, ph (079) 469 333, fax (079) 469 598.

Credit cards accepted: American Express, Visa, Diners Club, MasterCard and Bankcard.

DIVING

There is not much here for scuba divers, but the Resort arranges diving trips out to the Reef. Snorkelling trips to Hardy Lagoon take place several days a week.

HAMILTON ISLAND

Hamilton has an area of 6 sq km, and is home to the largest resort in the South Pacific with its own jet airport.

The resort was the brain-child of Gold Coast entrepreneur Keith Williams, with help from friends such as Ansett Airlines. He had originally leased the island for deer farming, but converted this lease to one for tourism.

The workmen moved onto the island in 1982; parts of the complex were operational by 1984; and the entire resort was completed before the end of 1986. All this without interference from the Green Movement, even when the 15-storey condos went up, and the airport runways were laid.

In the beginning it was a huge success, but disaster struck in ways that the management could neither foresee or control - firstly the domestic pilots' strike, then the international recession. Finally, in May 1992, Hamilton Island was placed in receivership, but in late 1993 it was successfully floated on the Australian Stock Exchange, and in March 1994 management of the resort was taken over by the Holiday Inn chain.

The resort is actually a small town with shops (including a supermarket and a TAB), restaurants and a 400 berth marina. There are a few walking tracks on the undeveloped parts of the island, and the main one leads up to Passage Peak (230m)

the highest point on the island. To get around the island there are a few choices. There is a taxi service, a radio controlled mini-bus service, or you can rent a golf buggy and drive yourself. Hamilton even has island bus tours that operate daily and cost around $15 per person.

There is an animal park at the northern end of the island, with native animals, crocodiles and performing cockatoos. Entry is $10 adult, $5 child.

Snorkelling off the island

HOW TO GET THERE

By Air

Ansett Australia has daily flights to Hamilton from Brisbane, Cairns and Sydney.

By Sea

Fantasea Cruises operate a service to Hamilton from Shute Harbour. See *Cruises* in Airlie Beach section.

ACCOMMODATION

There are several different types of accommodation from which to choose, all part of the **Resort**.

There are 51 Bures; 60 rooms in the Allamanda Lodge; 60 rooms in the Bougainvillea Lodge; 350 Premier Rooms in the Hamilton Towers; 168 apartments in the Whitsunday Towers; and 60 two-bedroom apartments in the lodges.

Resort facilities are: 8 freshwater swimming pools, 9 a la carte restaurants, 8 bars, 24 shops and boutiques, tennis courts, squash courts, gymnasium, aerobic classes, mini golf, live entertainment, parasailing, waterskiing, sailboards, SCUBA diving & lessons, catamarans, free Kids' Club.

Room facilities are: private balcony, air-conditioning, fans, tea/coffee making facilities, ironing facilities, refrigerator and mini bar, colour TV, IDD/STD telephone, hairdryer.

Tariffs for one night per person/twin share are:

Bure/Allamanda - $96

Bougainvillea - $146

Premier Room - $161

Whitsunday Towers - $165

2 bedroom Apartment - $220.

The above rates are room only, and include transfers from/to airport, beach and water volleyball, snorkelling lesson, pool SCUBA lessons and demonstration, children under 12 years eat free from kids' menu when dining with adults in Cascades Brasserie. Note that children 0 to 14 years stay free if sharing with adults and using existing bedding. All other activities, meals, drinks, etc. are at visitors' expense.

Maximum room capacity is Bure/Allamanda/Bougainvillea - 3; Premier-Whitsunday/2 Bedroom - 4.

Reservations can be made through any travel agent, or direct through Hamilton Island Resort, Private Mail Bag, Hamilton Island Post Office, 4803, ph (079) 469 999, fax (079) 468 888.

Credit cards accepted: All major cards.

DIVING

H2O Sportz, Front Street (PO Box 19) Hamilton Island, 4803, ph and fax (079) 469 888, is the only diving operation on Hamilton Island. A PADI 5-star Dive Centre, it has all the services expected of a top dive facility. There is a wide range of diving options ranging from half-day trips to nearby fringing reefs, day trips on specialist dive boats, and large catamarans that sail to the Outer Reef.

H2O Sportz offer daily trips to the Outer Barrier Reef and visits such sites as Hook, Hardy, Black and Bait Reefs and the Whitsunday Island area. These are all Marine National Parks and offer some of the best diving in the area.

LONG ISLAND

Long Island is separated from the mainland by a channel that is only 500m wide, making it the closest resort island to the Queensland coast. It has an area of 12 sq km, but is about 11km long, so it is apparent that it is extremely narrow, only about 1.5km at its widest.

The island was originally called Port Molle, named after the Lieutenant Governor of the colony of NSW from 1814, who had his name liberally sprinkled on islands in the area then even more than today. We still have North, Mid and South Molle, but there was also West Molle, which became Daydream, and this one whose name was changed to Long by

Matthew Flinders.

The first resorts opened in the 1930s; one at Happy Bay, the other at Palm Bay. The Happy Bay establishment lasted up to 1983 when new buyers changed the name to Whitsunday 100 and tried to make it into another Great Keppel, but without much success. It was taken over and refurbished by Contiki in 1986 for their 18 to 35 clientele, then in 1990 new owners thought the name "The Island" would catch on, but in 1991 it became the Radisson Long Island Resort, and in January 1994, Club Crocodile.

Palm Bay Resort, in the southern part of the island, was devastated by a cyclone in the mid-1970s, but is back in operation as the Palm Bay Hideaway a low-key, old fashioned resort without all the commercial razzle-dazzle.

There was another resort at Paradise Bay, on the southern tip of Long Island, but it has never seemed to have the appeal of the others and has opened and closed several times. At the time of going to press it was closed and on the market.

Long Island has 20km of bush walks through the National Park, and there are some nice sandy beaches on its western side, but at Happy Valley the tidal variations cause the water to be so far from the beach that it is easier to swim in the pool. Also, the box jellyfish makes its appearance in the vicinity from March to November. The beaches on the eastern side tend to be rocky and usually windy, but the dredging that has been done at Palm Bay makes it ideal for swimming, and for mooring yachts.

HOW TO GET THERE

From Proserpine the Sampsons Coach transfers visitors from the airport to Shute Harbour and connects with the water taxi to Long Island. Fares are: return coach - $26 adult, $13 child; return water taxi $22 adult, $12 child.

ACCOMMODATION

Club Crocodile, a sister to the Club Crocodile at Airlie Beach, has beachfront units (3-star) and garden view (2 1/2-star) units.

Resort facilities are: restaurants, cafe, bbq, two bars, two swimming pools, spa, sauna, tennis courts, dance club and bar, extensive range of watersports, gymnasium, paddleboards, catamaran, coral viewing, resort store, games room, Kids' Club, laundry/ironing facilities, EFTPOS.

Room facilities are: private bathroom, air-conditioning (Beachfront), refrigerator, tea/coffee making facilities, radio, colour TV, balcony, ceiling fans IDD/STD telephone, daily cleaning service.

Tariffs for one night per person/twin share are:
Garden (room only) - $69
Garden (dinner and breakfast) - $109
Beachfront (room only) - $84
Beachfront (dinner and breakfast) - $124.

Not included in the above rates are scuba diving, water taxi, fuel powered water sports or diving.

Reservations can be made through Australian Resorts, ph 008 812 525 (7 days), from overseas ph (+ 61 7) 360 2444, or through any Qantas office. They can also be made direct through Club Crocodile Long Island Resort, Long Island, via Shute Harbour, 4802, ph (079) 469 400, fax (079) 469 555.

Credit cards accepted: American Express, Bankcard, Visa, MasterCard, Diners Club.

Palm Bay Hideaway accommodation consists of cabins and bures.

Resort facilities are: catamarans, windsurfing, volleyball, snorkelling gear, paddle skis, bar, dining room, hand line fishing gear, bbq, swimming pool, spa, laundry/ironing facilities, lounge area, general store, outdoor dining terrace, tree house, open fireplace.

Room facilities are: private bathrooms, verandah, tea/coffee making facilities, ceiling fans, refrigerator, cooking facilities and utensils.

Tariffs for one night per person/twin share are:
Cabin (room only) - $98
Cabin (full board) - $150

Bure (room only) - $140
Bure (full board) - $193.

Not included in the above rates are the water taxi transfer or fuel powered water sports.

Reservations can be made through Australian Resorts, ph 008 812 525 (7 days), from overseas ph (+61 7) 360 2444, or through any Qantas office. They can also be made direct through Palm Bay Resort, Private Mail Bag 28, Mackay, 4740, ph (079) 469 233.

Credit cards accepted: Visa, MasterCard, Bankcard, American Express.

The resort shop has food supplies for those wishing to utilise the kitchen facilities, but it will obviously be much cheaper to take your own provisions.

DIVING

The Club Crocodile has a dive shop and can arrange trips out to the Reef.

SOUTH MOLLE ISLAND

South Molle has an area of 4 sq km, and is the largest of the Molle group. It is close to Mid Molle, and in fact you can walk from South Molle to Mid Molle at any time. Another island that is very close is Daydream.

With the oldest of the resorts in the Whitsunday Group, South Molle is mostly national park, and offers some good, if short, walks. The highest point is Mt Jeffreys, 198m, and it offers great views of the surrounding islands. Good views can also be seen from Balancing Rock and Spion Kop.

The first European settler was Henry George Lamond, who moved in with his wife and children in 1927 and stayed for ten years. There is a memorial to his son, Hal, on top of Lamond Hill.

South Molle is very much a family resort, there is even a pre-school nursery as well as activities for school age children.

HOW TO GET THERE

The choice is between launch transfer from Shute Harbour, or water taxi from Hamilton Island. See Airlie Beach *Cruises* section .

ACCOMMODATION

The **Resort** has six different categories of rooms, which are not the most modern, but are definitely comfortable. The Family rooms overlook the golf course, and have a double bedroom that can be shut off from the rest of the unit. They are ideal for a family of six.

Golf rooms also overlook the golf course and can accommodation a maximum of two.

Beachcomber units are freestanding and are located on the beachfront. They can accommodate a maximum of four.

Reef units are set back 30-40 metres from the beach in a garden setting, and are handy to all facilities. They can accommodate four.

Whitsunday units have prime beachfront locations, facing the Whitsunday passage. Ground floor rooms have patios and those on the first floor have balconies. They can accommodate a maximum of four.

Polynesian units are located on a hillside and have view overlooking the Whitsundays. They are 200m from the main resort area and can accommodate a maximum of four.

Resort facilities are: golf course, swimming pool, wading pool, kids' club, spa, sauna, beach towels, hairdresser, gift shop, coffee shop, live entertainment, disco, tennis, squash, volleyball, archery, gymnasium, snorkelling, scuba diving (tuition available), parasailing, water skiing, paddle skis, organised beach sports, windsurfers, catamarans, Great Barrier Reef cruises, day cruises to other islands, EFTPOS.

Room facilities are: private bathroom, ceiling fan, colour TV, refrigerator, IDD/STD phone, radio, tea/coffee making facilities, iron, ironing board, serviced daily.

Tariffs for one night per person/twin share are:
Family rooms - $180
Golf rooms - $180
Beachcomber units - $200
Reef units - $200
Whitsunday units - $215
Polynesian units - $200.

The above rates include all meals. They do not include golf balls, tennis balls, squash balls or fuel powered watersports.

Reservations can be made through Ansett Australia on ph 13 13 44 or direct through the resort, South Molle Island Resort, via Shute Harbour, 4802, ph (079) 469 433, fax (079) 469 580.

Credit cards accepted: All major cards.

A typical island in the Whitsunday group.

DIVING

There is a PADI dive school at the Resort and it offers short courses for beginners, and longer ones that lead to PADI accreditation. Contact the Resort for more information.

DAYDREAM ISLAND

Daydream is a small island with an area of just 17ha. It is a little over 1km long and no more than a couple of hundred metres at its widest point, but it has one of the largest resorts which is managed by the Travelodge chain.

Originally known as West Molle, the island is the closest resort island to Shute Harbour. It was first settled in the 1880s by graziers, but the first resort was opened by Paddy Murray, who had purchased the island in 1933 and changed its name to Daydream after his boat.

Reg Ansett (later Sir Reginald), of airline fame, bought the resort in 1947 and ran it until 1953 when he pulled the whole lot down and transferred it to Hayman Island.

In the mid-1960s, a resort was established under the leadership of Bernie Elsey and it operated until destroyed by a cyclone in 1970. During this time Daydream's reputation was anything but squeaky clean, but it could be that the 60s were not the time to introduce topless bathing or illegal gambling.

Now the resort is owned by the Jennings Group Ltd, which spent $100 million on a new complex at the northern end of the island and opened it in December 1990. Previous resorts had been at the southern end, but that part now has a Beach Club, with a nice sandy beach, a swimming pool, a bar, shops and a cafe. This is where all water activities are based, and the facilities can be used by resort guests and people on day trips from other islands and the mainland.

HOW TO GET THERE

Transfers are from the Daydream Island counter at Proserpine airport. A Daydream Island Coach will transfer guests to Shute Harbour to connect with the water taxi to the island. Fares are: return coach - $26 adult, $13 child; return water taxi $22 adult, $12 child.

ACCOMMODATION

Daydream Island Travelodge Resort accommodation is divided into three categories: Garden Room, which can accommodate up to 5 people; Oceanview Room, also accommodating 5; and Sunlover Room for 4 people.

Resort facilities are: 3 restaurants, bakery/coffee shop, 4 bars, live entertainment, disco, spas, sauna, 2 swimming pools, gymnasium, aerobics, tennis courts, windsurfing, catamaran sailing, paddle skis, snorkelling scuba diving and tuition, outer Reef excursions, waterskiing, paraflying, tour desk, laundry/ironing facilities, free child care (0-5 (9am-11pm daily), children's playground, Kids'Club (5-12 years - 9am-11pm daily).

Room facilities are: private bathrooms, mini bar, iron/board, hairdryer, tea/coffee making facilities, refrigerator, air-conditioning, colour TV, in-house movies, IDD/STD telephone, radio, daily cleaning service.

Tariffs for one night per person/twin share are:

Garden - $90

Oceanview - $105

Sunlover - $130.

The above rates are room only, but free meals are provided for children under three, and special $6 meals for those who are 3 to 14. Family room rates are available as well.

Also not included in the above rates are any sports that require fuel.

Reservations can be made Australian Resorts, ph 008 812 525 (7 days), from overseas ph (+ 61 7) 360 2444, or through any Qantas office. The Resort address is Daydream Island Travelodge Resort, Private Mail Bag 22, Mackay, 4740, ph (079) 488 488, fax (079) 488 499.

DIVING

Sunlover's Beach, at the north-eastern end of the island, behind the resort, has a 50m strip of sand and some good coral offshore for snorkellers. The Whitsunday tidal range does not affect Daydream as much as the other islands.

The Resort dive shop offers courses, and day cruises to Hardy Reef, about 50km offshore.

WHITSUNDAY ISLAND

Although Whitsunday is the largest of the island in the Whitsunday Group, it does not have a resort. But it does have Whitehaven Beach, the longest and best beach in the whole group. The destination for many cruises, there is good snorkelling off the southern end of the beach.

There are several camping sites on the island, and more information can be obtained from the QNP&WS at Airlie Beach.

HOOK ISLAND

Hook Island has an area of 53 sq km, some great beaches and some of the best diving sites in the Whitsundays, but it has one of the smallest resorts. The island is also home to an underwater observatory that has an abundance of colourful corals and marine life. Though with so many trips available to the Outer Reef and the modern semi-submersible craft that tour operators use, you have to wonder why anyone would want to visit an underwater observatory. Still, it is popular with many, and visitors who are part of a cruise do not have to pay the entry fee of $8.50 adult, $4.50 child.

Hook Island has two long, narrow bays on its southern end - Macona Inlet and Nara Inlet. Macona has a National Parks camping site, and Nara has caves with Aboriginal wall paintings.

There is a variety of wildlife on the island, but one that can prove quite pesky is the large goanna. These have been known to chew through canvas to get to campers' stores.

HOW TO GET THERE

Launch transfers from Shute Harbour cost $15 per person - see *Cruises* section in Airlie Beach.

ACCOMMODATION

The low-key **Resort** has only one style of accommodation - cabins, but in two sizes.

Resort facilities are: bar, coffee shop, gift shop, bbq area, paddle skis, on site scuba instructor.

Cabins have air conditioning and a refrigerator, but washroom, toilet and cooking facilities are all shared.

Tariff for one night per person/twin share is $19 in a 2 berth cabin, and $39 in a family cabin that will accommodate up to 6 people.

Reservations can be made through any of the Airlie Beach and Shute Harbour travel agents, or by contacting Ansett Australia on 13 13 44. The resort does not take bookings itself, but will provide information on (018) 775 142.

DIVING

The northern end of Hook Island has some good diving and snorkelling sites - Pinnacle Point, Manta Ray Bay, Butterfly Bay and Alcyonaria Point. The resort can organise reef trips.

HAYMAN ISLAND

Hayman Island has an area of 4 sq km, and is the most northerly of the Whitsunday resort islands. Its resort is one of the most luxurious on the Great Barrier Reef, and in fact is widely considered to be one of the top ten resorts in the world.

In 1866 the island was named after Thomas Hayman, navigator of the HMS *Salamander* which served in these waters for many years. In 1904 the island was leased by Thomas Abel for grazing his cattle, but he sold out in 1907.

The first resort was established in 1935 by Bert Hallam and his brother, but this was a simple affair for fishing trips.

Reginald Ansett took over the island in 1947, and the fishing resort closed its doors in 1948, then in 1950 the Hayman Resort opened and remained so until 1985 when it was closed for a multi-million dollar rebuild.

There are several bushwalks on Hayman, including an 8km circuit and walks to Blue Pearl Bay or Dolphin Point. It is also possible to walk to nearby Arkhurst Island at low tide.

HOW TO GET THERE

Ansett Australia flies to Hamilton Island and visitors can be transferred from there, but arrangements must be made for the transfer when booking the flight.

Visitors can also be transported from Airlie Beach - see *Cruises* in Airlie Beach Section - $40 return adult, $20 return child 3-14.

ACCOMMODATION

Hayman Island Resort offers luxury to the nth degree. There are antiques and treasures from around the world, as well as Australian works of art throughout the resort. There are six categories of accommodation: Palm Garden View Rooms - maximum 2 persons; Beachfront Rooms - maximum 2 persons; West Wing Rooms - maximum 3 persons; West Wing Suites - maximum 3 persons; East Wing Rooms - maximum 3 persons; East Wing Suites - maximum 4 persons.

Resort facilities are: six restaurants, cocktail bars, entertainment, pool bar, saltwater swimming pool, 2 freshwater pools, fully equipped health club, beauty salon, hairdresser, snorkelling, hobie cat sailing, windsurfing, beach volleyball, paddle skis, full and half court tennis, golf target range, lawn croquet, walking tracks, putting green, outdoor jacuzzi/spa, billiards room, table tennis, card and games room, badminton, new release movies on big screen, parasailing, waterskiing, water sleigh, yacht charter, Reef trips, dinghy hire, snorkelling excursions/picnics, tennis coaching, game/bottom and reef fishing trips, EFTPOS.

Rooms facilities are: air conditioning, ceiling fan, colour TV, video, IDD/STD telephone, hairdryer, mini bar, bathrobes, room safe, serviced daily.

Tariffs for one night per person/twin share are:

Palm Garden View Rooms - $198

Beachfront Rooms - $275

West Wing Rooms - $295

West Wing Suites - $550

East Wing Rooms - $325

East Wing Suites - $650.

The above rates are room only - meals are not included, and they don't come cheap either. The wine list is extensive, and of course, expensive.

Activities not included in the rates are: parasailing, water skiing, water sleigh, yacht charter, Reef trips, dinghy hire, snorkelling excursions/picnics, tennis coaching, game/bottom and reef fishing trips.

Reservations can be made through Ansett Australia, ph 13 13 44, through the resort direct, Hayman Island Resort, Hayman Island, 4801, ph (079) 469 100, fax (079) 469 410, or through any travel agent.

Credit cards accepted: All major cards.

DIVING

Hayman is closer to the outer Reef than other resort islands, and Hayman has a full-time dive boat, so what more could a diver want. Thirty kilometres north-east of Hayman are Hardy and Black Reefs.

CENTRAL BARRIER REEF

TOWNSVILLE

Townsville has a population of around 130,000, and is the second largest city in Queensland and the main commercial centre of northern Queensland. It offers not only easy access to the attractions of the Magnetic North and the Great Barrier Reef, but also all of the facilities of a major city.

Careful zoning has ensured that the city retains much of its original architecture and character. A walk around town will show you what makes North Queensland so different. Old wooden, high-set houses stand everywhere, built to allow cooling breezes under the house, and to provide a refuge during the heat of the day. In the gardens mango, pawpaw (papaya) and banana trees seem exotic to the visitor, but are the normal homegrown product of the Townsville backyard.

Townsville is also a busy port that services Mt Isa, southern cities and south-east Asia. It has two metal refineries and other industrial enterprises.

CLIMATE

Average temperatures: January max 31C (88F) - min 24C (75F) and high humidity; July max 25C (77F) - min 15C (59F). Average annual rainfall is 1194mm - wettest months January-March, with an average of 873mm.

HOW TO GET THERE

By Air

Qantas has three daily direct flights from Brisbane to Townsville, and flights from other capital cities connect with them.

Ansett Australia has several daily flights, and these also connect with flights from other cities in Australia.

By Bus

McCafferty's Coaches and Greyhound/Pioneer have daily services to Townsville from Brisbane and Cairns.

By Rail

The *Sunlander* leaves Brisbane at 10am on Tues, Thurs & Sat and arrives in Townsville at 10.20am the next day.

The *Queenslander* (1st Class) and the *Spirit of the Tropics* (Economy Class) leaves Brisbane at 10am on Sun and arrives in Townsville at 10.20am on Mon. Obviously, these are two different parts of the same train, but note that passengers cannot pass from one class to the other.

By Road

From Brisbane via the Bruce Highway, 1380km. Townsville is 374km south of Cairns.

TOURIST INFORMATION

Townsville Enterprise Limited is in Enterprise House, 3 The Strand, Townsville, ph (077) 713 061.

The Townsville Information Centre is on the Bruce Highway at the southern approach to the city. Open daily 9am-5pm, the centre has information and maps on both the city of Townsville and the North Queensland region.

There is also the Coppertop Information Kiosk in Flinders Mall.

ACCOMMODATION

Here is a selection of available accommodation with prices for a double room per night, which should be used as a guide only. The telephone area code is 077.

Sheraton Breakwater Casino Hotel, Sir Leslie Thiess Drive, ph 222 333 - 193 rooms, 2 licensed restaurants, bars, swimming pool, spa, sauna, gym, tennis courts, casino - $195.

Townsville Travelodge, 334 Flinders Mall, ph 722 477 - 134 rooms, 2 licensed restaurants, bars, swimming pool - $130.

Aquarius on the Beach, 75 The Strand, ph 724 255 - all suite hotel, full kitchenette - licensed restaurant, bar, cafe, swimming pool - $110.

Reef International Hotel, 63-64 The Strand, ph 211 777 - 45 rooms, licensed restaurant, swimming pool, spa - $95-105.

Southbank Motor Inn, 23-29 Palmer Street, ph 211 474 - 98 rooms, licensed restaurant - $79.

Seagulls Resort, 74 The Esplanade, ph 213 111 - 70 rooms, licensed restaurant, 2 swimming pools, tennis - $78.

Colonial Gardens Resort, Woolcock Street, ph 252 222 - licensed restaurant, swimming pool, sauna, spa - $69.

Cleveland Hotel on the Mall, 409 Flinders Street, ph 721 888 - 5-storeys, licensed bar, coffee shop - $66.

Historic Yongala Lodge, 11 Fryer Street, North Ward, ph 724 633 - 9 rooms, licensed restaurant, swimming pool - $59.

Aitkenvale Motel, 224 Ross River Road, Aitkenvale, ph 752 444 - 28 rooms, licensed restaurant, swimming pool - $58.

Casino City Motor Inn, 100 Bowen Road, Rosslea, ph 754 444 - 17 rooms, BYO restaurant, swimming pool - $56.

Caravan Parks

Sun City Caravan Park, 119 Bowen Road, Rosslea, ph 757 733 - powered sites $12 x 2; tent sites $12 x 2; cabins $39 x 2.

Big 4 Woodlands, Bruce Highway North, ph 516 955 - powered sites (ensuite) $15.50 x 2; cabins $43 x 2.

Coonambelah Caravan Park, 547 Ingham Road, ph 745 205 - powered sites $13 x 2; tent sites $11 x 2; on-site vans $25-35 x 2; cabins $25-38 x 2.

Showgrounds Caravan Park, 16 Kings Road, West End, ph 721 487 - powered sites $12 x 2; tent sites $10 x 2; on-site vans $25 x 2; cabins $40-45 x 2.

EATING OUT

Townsville has many hotels serving counter lunches, takeaway shops and good restaurants. The international hotels have at least one restaurant, and the staff where you are staying can probably recommend a restaurant - based on price or cuisine. Here are a few that you might like to try.

Affaire de Coeur, 1 Sturt Street, ph 722 742 - Licensed - seafood - open for dinner Mon-Sat, lunch Mon-Fri.

Cobbers Restaurant & Take-Away, Upstairs Northtown, ph 712 351 - Licensed - a la carte menu - open for lunch Mon-Fri, dinner Fri-Sat with special price for 3 course dinner and show on Sat.

Down Under Restaurant, Dal Roberts Arcade, Flinders Mall, ph 723 838 - Licensed - a la carte restaurant - open for lunch Mon-Fri, dinner Fri-Sat.

Le Boulevard Brasserie Restaurant, 215 Flinders Street East, ph 714 393 - Licensed - classic French and seafood - open for dinner Tues-Sun.

Dynasty Chinese Seafood Restaurant, 288 Flinders Street, ph 727 099 - Licensed - open for lunch Mon-Sat, dinner nightly - silver service.

Capitol Chinese Restaurant & Takeaway, 189 Flinders Street, ph 713 838 - Licensed - open daily - two sections, one banquet based, the other seafood with a smorgasbord on Sunday.

Pasinis North Italian Restaurant, 2 Archer Street South, ph 716 333 - BYO - homemade pasta, alfresco dining - open for dinner Mon-Sat.

Bananas Rock Cafe, 141 Flinders Street, ph 712 799 - BYO - budget priced steak, pasta and salad - open Sun-Thurs 6pm-4am, Fri-Sat 6pm-6am.

Pizza Hut, Charters Towers Road, Hyde Park, ph 722 944; Fulham Road, Vincent Village, ph 752 222.

KFC, Hermit Park; Garbutt; Cranbrook.

McDonald's, Aitkenvale and The Lakes.

ENTERTAINMENT

First and foremost in this category would have to be the *Sheraton Breakwater Casino* in Sir Leslie Thiess Drive, ph 222

333. It is open Sun-Thurs 10am-2am, Fir-Sat 10am-4am and dress regulations apply. Games are: Blackjack, Roulette, Baccarat, Sheraton Wheel, Two-up, Keno, Mini dice, Craps, Sic-bo, Video and Poker machines. Of course, players must be over 18 years of age.

For the less adventurous who want to hang on to their holiday dollar, Townsville's cinema complex, *Townsville 5*, is in Sturt Street. Contact 714 101 for current programs.

Townsville Civic Theatre is in Boundary Street, South Townsville, ph 714 188, and can seat 1066 people. It offers culturally diverse programs, as does the Dean Park *Soundshell*, an outdoor venue with capacity for 5000.

The *Entertainment Centre* on Sir Leslie Thiess Drive is primarily for indoor sport, such as basketball, but if a big-name performer or band hits town that is where the concert will be.

Fisherman's Wharf in Ogden Street, ph 211 838, has live entertainment seven nights a week, a restaurant, coffee shop and a bar.

If you are in the mood for dancing, head for Flinders Street East where there are a few night clubs, including *The Bank* and *Bullwinkles*, and around the corner in The Strand is the *Criterian*.

For a pub night out try *The Australian* in Palmer Street or the *Great Northern* in Flinders Street West.

The Marina with the Sheraton Hotel in the background, Townsville.

SHOPPING

Flinders Street Mall has several boutiques and specialty shops and *Northtown on the Mall*, but the big shopping centres are out of town.

At Aitkenville, 20 minutes from the city centre is *Stockland* which has David Jones department stores as well as specialty shops, and across the road is *K-Mart Plaza* which has food shops and, of course, K-Mart.

The suburb of Hyde Park has *Castletown* which has a variety of chain stores, including Target, and the suburb of Kirwan and *The Willows*.

North Queensland's largest arts and crafts market is held in Flinders Mall every Sunday 8.30am-12.30pm. Called *Cotters Market* it has pottery, jewellery, paintings, leadlighting, leatherwork, woodwork, crocheting and knitwear, original handicrafts, wooden toys, hats, homemade goodies, plants and preserves, islander crafts, timber fishing lures, homemade chocolates, Devonshire teas, orchids, souvenirs, seasonal fruit and vegies, and what more could you want? For more info phone (077) 220 380.

SIGHTSEEING

Castle Hill (286m) offers a panoramic view of Townsville. It is topped by an octagonal restaurant that commands a 260 degree view of the city and the bay. Nearby Mt Stuart is also an excellent vantage point.

Flinders Mall is virtually in the heart of the city. It is a landscaped pedestrian mall with a relaxed atmosphere. The *Perc Tucker Regional Gallery* is in the mall, ph (077) 220 289, and it houses an extensive collection of national and regional art in an impressive building that was originally a bank. It is open Tues-Thurs and Sat 10am-5pm, Fri 2-9pm, Sun 10am-1pm and admission is free. Nearby is *St Joseph's Cathedral* in Fryer Street, a reflection of the architecture of the past.

The Strand, Townsville's sea promenade, has many parks including the *Sister Kenny Park* and the *Anzac Memorial Park* with its Centenary Fountains, waterfall and bougainvillea gardens. Also along the Strand is the *Tobruk Memorial Swimming Pool*.

Queen's Gardens, next to Queens's Park, encompass Kissing Point and Jezzine Army Barracks. The barracks have a military museum. An all-tide rock swimming pool, a restaurant and a kiosk are also in the gardens.

Town Common Environmental Park, Cape Pallarenda, is a flora and fauna sanctuary where visitors may see some rare water fowl, including the primitive magpie goose. In the winter months, at the heights of the dry season, as many as 3000 brolgas, along with up to 180 other species of bird, flock to the Common's salt-marsh lagoons and water-holes. The brolga is famous for its courting ritual, and the park provides visitors with an excellent opportunity to see this dance at close quarters. The park is open daily 6.30am-6.30pm and barbecue facilities are available.

Great Barrier Reef Wonderland, 2-86 Flinders Street East, is open daily 9am-5pm and is one of the most popular attractions in Townsville. It features the Great Barrier Reef Aquarium, the world's largest living coral reef aquarium. Conceived and operated by the Great Barrier Reef Marine Park Authority, the aquarium includes a huge main tank containing a living coral reef, a smaller tank displaying sharks and other reef predators, and an extensive area containing numerous display tanks, educational exhibits, a theatrette and a large touch tank. Visitors can walk beneath the water through a transparent tunnel surrounded by hundreds of coral reef animals.

Wonderland also includes the *Omnimax Theatre*, which is dome-shaped and uses a special type of projection so that the image is above and around the audience - a fascinating experience. The theatre seats 200 people, and has facilities for the disabled.

The *Museum of Tropical Queensland*, a branch of the Queensland Museum, is also at Wonderland. It has the world's best collection of Australian dinosaur bones, and a very interesting display called "Queensland in the Age of Reptiles". Very popular with visitors are the stories of the environment from an indigenous perspective told by local Aboriginal people.

Wonderland also houses: the operational headquarters of the Great Barrier Reef Marine Park Authority, the federal government agency responsible for safeguarding the Great Barrier Reef Marine Park; a licensed restaurant featuring tropical cuisine; a shop with a variety of souvenirs and educational material; a post office; and an information centre, run by the Queensland Department of Environment and Heritage with all you need to know about national parks, marine national parks, camping permits and locations, walking trails, and wildlife.

From the Wonderland's ferry terminal cruises depart throughout the day to Magnetic Island and the Outer Barrier Reef.

Admission to the Aquarium is $10 adult, $5 child (4-14), $26 family, ph (077) 818 886; to the Omnimax Theatre $9.50 adult, $4.75 child (4-14); to the Museum of Tropical Queensland $2.50 adult, $1.25 child (4.14). The Wonderland bus will pick up from hotels and motels for the trip to the complex, ph (077) 757 333 to make arrangements.

South of Townsville, in fact much closer to the town of Ayr, the wreck of *Yongala* lies of Cape Bowling Green. A coastal steamer, she was bound for Cairns when a cyclone struck on March 14, 1911, and she went down with all hands - 121 people including officers and crew. The wreck was discovered in 1958, but has only been dived regularly since the 1980s.

Diving the *Yongala* is rated as one of the best wreck-dive experiences in the world. The wreck is 110m long, and supports a system of hard and soft corals and many different marine animals including pelagics, stingrays, gropers, turtles and sea snakes. She lies in 30m of water with her funnel only 15m below the surface. The *Yongala* is protected by the historic shipwreck act as a memorial to all who went down with her, so nothing may be taken from the ship. This is a temptation as there are dinner plates, knives, forks, and some evidence of human remains, but where they are they must stay. See the

Scuba Diving section under *Sport* for operators who will take divers to the wreck.

SPORT

Swimming

There are three salt water mesh swimming enclosures: one at *Rowes Bay*, one at *Pallarenda*, and one next to the rock pool in Queen's Gardens. They provide safe sea swimming, free from sharks, sea stingers and other marine hazards.

Golf

Townsville Golf Club, Benson Street, Rosslea, ph (077) 790 133 - 27-hole championship course - equipment hire - open 6.30am-6pm club house open 10am-8pm.

Rowes Bay Golf Club, Heatley Parade, Pallarenda, ph (077) 741 188 - 18-hole par 72 course. - equipment hire - open seven days.

Willows Golf Club, 19th Avenue, Kirwan, ph (077) 734 352 - 18-hole course - open daily.

Horse Riding

Ranchlands Equestrian Centre, 83 Hammond Way, Kelso, ph (077) 740 124 - open week days and nights.

Range View Ranch, Thorntons Gap Road, Hervey's Range, ph (077) 780 120 - horse hire, camping, bushwalking and weekend trail rides - open weekends and public holidays.

Saddle Sense Riding School, 95 Haynes Road, Jensen, ph (077) 516 372 - trail rides and camping - open Wed-Sun.

Fishing/Yacht Charters

Australian Pacific Charters, 792 Flinders Street, ph (077) 712 534 - 1 day reef trip departs 6am Tues & Sun, fishing gear included - from $120; 2 day reef trip departs 9pm Fri, air conditioned accommodation, meals, fishing gear - from $250.

Coral Sea Fishing Charters, 4 Dahl Crescent, Wulguru, ph (077)

781 950 - reef fishing trips; light tackle game fishing to Cape Bowling Green; giant marlin at Lizard Island/Cairns - 40 ft O'Brien boat - from $1000 per day.

Farr Better Yacht Charters, 76 Allen Street, South Townsville, ph (077) 716 294 - yacht and boat charter - bare boat or with sail guide - Hood 23ft yacht and *Farr Star* 40ft yacht - sailing training (AF) - 7 days - from $150-450 per day. Special weekend trips to Palm and Dunk Islands.

Tangaroa Cruises, 19 Crowle Street, Hyde Park, ph (077) 798 155 - 50ft motor cruiser available for extended cruises, social outings, fishing and diving trips - support vessel - POA.

True Blue Charters, 65 Gilbert Crescent, Yarrawonga, ph (077) 715 474 - charter boat for reef and game fishing, diving, snorkelling, island cruising, etc - maximum 8 passengers - from $920 per day full boat charter - half day and other charters on request.

Scuba Diving/Courses

Mike Ball Dive Expeditions, 252 Walker Street, ph (077) 723 022 - internationally acclaimed 5 star PADI dive centre providing PADI instruction from entry level to Dive career programs - expeditions to Yongala wreck and Coral Sea, also Cod Hole - open Mon-Fri 8.45am-5pm, Sat 8.45am-noon - $350-450 Open water.

The Dive Bell, Shop 5, 141 Ingham Road, ph 211 155 - sport diving and dive shop - commercial diving school - diving trips to Yongala wreck and the reef - open Mon-Fri 8.30am-5pm, Sat 9am-noon - from $380 open water course.

Pro-Dive Townsville, shop 3, Great Barrier Reef Wonderland, Flinders Street East - PADI scuba diving school - 5 star Gold dive shop - charter boars, hire equipment, Yongala wreck dives - open daily 9am-5pm - from $385 learn to dive, $295 Yongala Wreck 3 days.

Skydiving/Parachuting

Townsville Parachute & Skydiving Centre, Lot 6 Skydiver Road, Manton, via Woodstock, ph (077) 215 346 - all sorts of jumps for beginners and experienced - kiosk, souvenirs, T-shirts, certificates - $280 tandem and static line course, $400 AFF Freefall course, $4 per night bunkhouse/camping.

TOURS

Detours, Shop 5, Great Barrier Reef Wonderland Complex, ph (077) 215 977, offer:

Rainforest Waterfalls - Butterfly display, Crystal Creek rainforest walk, fruit farm - 8 hours - $48 adult, $22 child - Tues, Thurs, Sat 9am.

Golden Outback - Charters Towers and outback country - 8 hours - $48 adult, $22 child - Mon, Wed, Fri 9am.

Billabong Sanctuary - wildlife sanctuary - 3 1/2 hours - $23 adult, $9 child (includes entrance fee) - 10am daily.

City Tour - 2 hours - $14 adult, $9 child - 11am daily.

Dunk Island - Mission Beach and cruise to Dunk - 12 hours - $67 adult, $27 child - Tues, Thurs, Sat, Sun 6.30am.

Dunk & Bedarra Islands - Same as Dunk Island + lunch, Bedarra Island, boom netting tropical fruit tasting - $87 adult, $39 child - Tues, Thurs, Sat, Sun 6.30am.

Ringtail Tours, PO Box 319, Aitkenvale, 4814, ph (077) 755 719, offer:

Coastal Connection - one way Townsville/Cairns, Cairns Townsville coach tour includes 2 nights accommodation, all meals, Kuranda rail, Lake Barrine cruise, forest walks, water falls, Mission Beach, qualified Biologist, $475 twin, $540 single, $330 child - Wed (Townsville), Sat (Cairns) 8.30am.

Pure Pleasure Tours, Breakwater Terminal, Sir Leslie Thiess Drive, ph (077) 213 555, offer:

City Sights Tour - 2 1/2 hours - $15 adult, $10 child - Mon-Sat 9.30am.

Billabong Bound - wildlife sanctuary + Devonshire tea - $25 adult, $12 child - 1pm daily.

King of Copper - tour of copper smelter, Devonshire tea at Billabong Sanctuary - $25 adult, $12 child - Mon, Wed 1pm from Great Barrier Reef Wonderland.

Aboriginal Art, Marine Science & Bush Tucker - full day - Australian Institute of Marine Science, Aboriginal guide, food gathering and cave art + Devonshire tea & picnic lunch - $65 adult, $35 child - Fri 9am-5pm.

Gold Rush Tour - Charters Towers + lunch & morning tea - $55 adult, $35 child - Mon, Fri 9am-5pm from Great Barrier Reef Wonderland.

World Heritage Rainforest - Rainforest at Mt Spec, tropical fruit farm, Cotters Market Sun, lunch & afternoon tea - $55 adult, $35 child - Wed, Sun 9am-5pm from Great Barrier Reef Wonderland.

City Airport Express - meets every flight - $5 single/$8 return adult, $3/$5 child.

Townsville from the air.

Kangaroo Tours, PO Box 1651, ph (077) 804 740, offer:
Lunch with Kangaroos - bush picnic, scenic tour, swim, Aussie bbq with damper and billy tea - $38.

CRUISES

Coral Princess Cruises, Level 1, Suite 2, Breakwater Marina, ph (077) 211 673, offer:
Cairns/Barrier Reef - 4 days/3 nights Barrier Reef and Island cruise - departs Townsville Tues 1pm - calls at resorts, uninhabited islands and reef - from $870 adult, $260 child.
Barrier Reef/Islands/Townsville - 4 days/3 nights resorts, reef islands to Townsville - departs Cairns Sat 9.30am - fares as above. Options include 4 days Cairns/Cairns including flight to Townsville, 2 days drop off Dunk Island, 7 day cruise return trip.

Magnetic Link Ferry Service, Great Barrier Reef Wonderland, ph (077) 211 913, offer:
Cruise to Magnetic Island - open return ticket, free pick up from accommodation - bus or mokes available - $15 adult, $7 child.
Magnetic Island Cruise/Bus - open duration, pick up from accommodation, cruise and bus tour of island with commentary, exploring and swimming - $20 adult, $9 child.
Cruise/Bus/Lunch Tour - return ticket, bus tour with commentary, poolside lunch at resort, use of facilities, accommodation pick up, morning departure - $29.50 adult, $14 child.
Cruise/Bus/Koala Park/Lunch - as above plus visit to Koala Park - $36.50 adult, $17 child.
Seafood Cruise - departs Wonderland 7.30pm, returns 10.30pm - seafood buffet, entertainment/dancing, bar - $25.50 adult, $15 child.
Harbour Lights Cruise - departs Quarterdeck Tavern 7pm for 2 hour cruise of harbour lights of Townsville, bar nibbles, entertainment - $5.

Magnetic Marine. Breakwater Terminal, Sir Leslie Thiess Drive, ph (077) 727 122, offer:
Magnetic Island Cruise - open return, ten departures daily, free

pick up from accommodation - $15 adult, $7 child.

Cruise/Bus tour - includes return ticket, unlimited bus travel on island, morning tea on ferry, free accommodation pick ups (guided bus tour $2 upgrade) - $20 adult, $10 child.

Cruise/Bus/Lunch - includes return ticket, unlimited bus travel, lunch at large choice of restaurants, free pick ups, morning tea on ferry (guided bus tour $2 upgrade) - $33 adult, $16 child, $80 family (2 + 2).

Pure Pleasure Cruises, Breakwater Terminal, Sir Leslie Thiess Drive, ph (077) 213 555, offer:

Kelso Outer Reef Tour - 50 nautical miles north to Kelso reef - includes swimming, snorkelling, fishing, glass bottom boat, buffet lunch, morning/afternoon tea all inclusive, bar and diving extra - $105 adult, $50 child, $250 family - departs 9am daily.

AIR CHARTERS

Townsville Helicopters, Townsville Airport, Garbutt, ph (077) 721 826 - $25 for 10 minutes, $420 per hour - 3 passengers.

Paterson Helicopters, c/- Townsville Aero Club, Townsville Airport, ph (077) 792 069 - helicopter service, joy flights charter, daylight hours - $250 per hour.

Townsville Aero Club, Townsville Airport, Garbutt, ph (077) 792 069 - aircraft charter, joy flights, aerial tours, flying training - prices on application.

Inland Pacific Air, Townsville Airport, Garbutt, ph (077) 752 044 - twin engine aircraft charter 4 to 11 seats - 7 aircraft available including pressurised executive Cessna - available all hours to any destination - prices on application.

Skygold Aviation, Hangar 117, Townsville Airport, Garbutt, ph 757 400 - aircraft charter, joy flights, aerial tours, flying training - destination as required - prices on application.

Townsville Air Tours, 5 Noonan Street, Garbutt, ph 018 779 597 - scenic flights over city, reef and islands - charter minimum 2 people - from $50.

MAGNETIC ISLAND

Magnetic Island has an area of 52 sq km and a permanent population of 1500. With 16 beaches, plenty of reasonably-priced accommodation, and an ideal climate, Magnetic is one of the most popular islands on the Reef.

Roughly triangular in shape, and misnamed by Captain Cook who thought the island had interfered with his compass, Magnetic's first European settlers were timber cutters at Nelly Bay in the early 1870s. A permanent settlement was not established until 1887 when Harry Butler and his family arrived at Picnic Bay. It was these people who began the tourist industry on the island and their story is told in *The Real Magnetic* by Jessie Macqueen, who was also one of the early settlers.

At the end of the century Robert Hayles built a hotel at Picnic Point and introduced a ferry service to the island on an old Sydney Harbour ferry, *The Bee*.

Magnetic Island now has several small towns, an aquarium and a koala sanctuary, but 70% of the island is national park. Box jellyfish are present around Magnetic between October and April, so during this time it is wise to swim only in the netted areas at Picnic Bay and Alma Bay.

The north coast of Magnetic is zoned Marine Park B, so fishing is not permitted.

There are quite a few good diving locations on the island's southern and eastern shores.

HOW TO GET THERE

Magnetic Link Ferry Service, ph (077) 211 913, and *Magnetic Marine*, ph (077) 727 122, run ferry services between Townsville and Magnetic Island, and their routes and prices are detailed in the *Cruises* section of Townsville in this chapter. The trip across Cleveland Bay from Townsville to Picnic Bay takes 20 minutes, then some of Magnetic Marine ferries continue on to Arcadia.

Capricorn Barge Company, ph (077) 725 422, run a car ferry to

Arcadia from the south side of Ross Creek, but, unless you are staying on the island for an extended period, a car is not really necessary.

TOURIST INFORMATION

The travel agent on the pier in Picnic Bay, (077) 785 155, knows everything there is to know about Magnetic Island, and has some helpful brochures. He can also look after all your tour booking, accommodation, vehicle hire and all travel arrangements.

The QNP&WS also has an office in Picnic Bay and can advise on the 22km of walking tracks on the island, and the best way to climb Mt Cook (497m).

ACCOMMODATION

The telephone area code is 077.

Hotels/Motels

The following prices are for a double room per night, and should be used as a guide only.

Tropical Palms Inn, 34 Picnic Street, Picnic Bay, ph 785 076 - 2 storey, air conditioned, TV/Video, tea/coffee making, kitchen facilities, bbq, swimming pool, shopping mall, vehicle hire - from $58 (from $395 per week - cottages from $325 per week).

Picnic Bay Holiday Hotel, 1 The Esplanade, Picnic Bay, ph 785 166 - 20 rooms with fans, licensed garden bistro, swimming pool, bbq - motel $39; lodge $49; family $55 (cooking facilities).

Arcadia Hotel Resort, 7 Marine Parade, Arcadia, ph 785 177 - 27 units, air conditioning, licensed restaurant, bistro, bar, swimming pools, spa, dive centre, shops - garden $75; Terrace $85.

Self-contained Units

Arcadia

Prices shown are for unit rental, and should be used as a guide only.

Dandaloo Gardens, 40-42 Hayles Avenue, Arcadia - 8 units each accommodating 5 per unit - 200m from PO, fans, balcony, colour TV, playground, swimming pool, sporting facilities, full kitchen, bbq - $75 per night, $495 per week.

Magnetic Haven, 7-9 Rheuben Terrace, Arcadia, ph 785 824 - 7 units accommodating 6 in 2 bedrooms, 8 in 3 bedrooms - 300m from PO, fans, balcony, colour TV/video, swimming pool, playground, spa, full kitchen facilities, bbq - from $65 per night, from $425 per week.

Arcadia Beach Apartments, 37 Marine Parade, Arcadia, ph 785 333 - 3 units each accommodating 5-7 people - 250m from PO, fans, balcony, colour TV, playground, swimming pool, full kitchen facilities, bbq - $490 per week.

Arcadia Palms, 20 Hayles Avenue, Arcadia, ph 785 077 - 2 x 2 bed room units accommodating 4-5 each - fans, screens, air conditioning, full kitchen facilities, microwave, colour TV, swimming pool - $70 per night.

Balandool, 5 Cook Road, Arcadia, ph 785 077 - 2 x 2 bed room units accommodating 4-5 each - near beach, fans (air conditioning in 1 unit), full kitchen facilities, colour TV - $350 per week.

Beachcomber Units, 12 Marine Parade, Arcadia, ph 725 333 - 2 bedroom units each accommodating 6 people - 150m from PO, opposite beach, air conditioning and fans, colour TV, playground, full kitchen facilities - $490 per week.

Brooke Haven, 5 Hordern Avenue, Arcadia, ph 785 262 - 3 units each accommodating 5 people - fans, colour TV, playground, swimming pool, spa, full kitchen facilities, bbq - $55-65 per night, $330-390 per week.

Butlers House, 33 Marine Parade, Arcadia, ph 785 333 - 2 bedroom house accommodating 6 people - 200m from PO, opposite beach, fans, balcony, colour TV, playground, full kitchen facilities - $490 per week.

Caversham Units, 26 Armand Way, Arcadia, ph 785 333 - 3 townhouses each accommodating 5 (1 double, 3 single beds) - close to Alma Beach, fans, TV, full kitchen facilities, close to PO and shops - $350 per week.

Nelly Bay

Camlachie Holiday Units, 122 Sooning Street, Nelly Bay, ph 785 499 - 2 units each accommodating 6 people - ocean views, set in natural bushland, front and rear patios, bbq area - minutes walk to pool, park, beach, playground, shops - $50 per night (min 2 nights), $240 per week.

Island Leisure Resort, 4 Kelly Street, Nelly Bay, ph 785 511 - 17 units each accommodating 5 people - 30m from beach, new bures, village garden setting, fans, patio, colour TV/video, tennis/night lights, swimming pool, spa, games room, kiosk, gym, bbq, full kitchen facilities - $84 per night, $504 per week.

Palm View, 114 Sooning Street, Nelly Bay, ph 785 596 - 9 units each accommodating 6, a house accommodating 10 - 530m from PO, fans, balcony, colour TV, swimming pool, spa, full kitchen facilities, bbq, shop - $75 per night, $490 per week (house $750 per week).

Alcoota, 14 Colleen Street, Nelly Bay, ph 785 077 - 2 units each accommodating 5 people (2 bedrooms) - 1km from PO, fans, colour TV, full kitchen facilities, bbq - $50 per night, $260 per week.

Anchorage, 110 Sooning Street, Nelly Bay, ph 785 596 - 3 units each accommodating 4-6 people - 500m from PO, air conditioning, fans, balcony, colour TV, bbq, playground, swimming pool, spa, full kitchen facilities - $70-80 per night, $484-525 per week.

Magnetic Island

Baringa Holiday Units, 15 Warboys Street, Nelly Bay, ph 785 367 - 2 units each accommodating 4 people - fans, swimming pool, sporting facilities, full kitchen facilities, bbq, colour TV, 200m supermarket, 50m opposite beach - $50 per night (min 3 nights), $300 per week.

Beachside Palm Units, 7 The Esplanade, Nelly Bay, ph 227 009 - 4 units each accommodating 5 people - 2 storeys, air conditioning, fans, balcony, colour TV, swimming pool, full kitchen facilities - $260 per week (1 bed), $360 per week (2 bed).

Horseshoe Bay

Coolawin Holiday Units, 13 Pacific Drive, Horseshoe Bay, ph 785 117 - 8 units - fully self contained - 1 bedroom sleeps 2 to 3, double bed with ensuite - 2 bedroom sleeps 4 to 5, double + 2 single beds and divan - $49-89 per night, $310-525 per week, depending on the time of the year.

Budget & Backpackers

Centaur House, 27 Marine Parade, Arcadia, ph 785 668 - 2 storeys, 7 rooms - 5km from PO, non-smoking units, sporting facilities, free tea/coffee, communal bath facilities, kitchen, laundry, bbq, bike hire - double/twin $34, dormitory $14.

Foresthaven Backpacker, 11 Cook Street, Arcadia, ph 785 153 - 25 rooms - fans, linen hire, bbq, colour TV lounge, playground, sporting facilities, communal bath, kitchen laundry, bike hire - single $26, twin $28, bunkhouse $12.

Sharkworld Resort, Nelly Bay Beachfront, ph 785 777 - 49 rooms - 1km from PO, fans, linen hire, licensed restaurant, entertainment, colour TV/video lounge, swimming pool, sporting facilities, communal bath, kitchen, bbq, shop - single $12, twin $24, bunkhouse $10, camping $7.

Magnetic Island Tropical Resort, Yates Street, Nelly Bay, ph 785 955 - swimming pool, spa, budget bistro breakfast, lunch and dinner, island tours, diving, horse riding - ensuite cabin $40, deluxe $50; camping $6 pp/pn.

Geoff's Place, 40 Horseshoe Bay Road, Horseshoe Bay, ph 785 577 - 30 rooms - 4km from PO, fans, linen hire, licensed restaurant, swimming pool, colour TV/video lounge, sporting facilities, spa, communal bath, kitchen, shop, bike hire - single $12, twin $15, marquee $8, camping $6, ensuite cabins with air conditioning and full service - $48 per night.

Hideaway Hostel, 32 Picnic Street, Picnic Bay, ph 785 110 - 16 rooms, no dorms - 100m from PO, fans, free linen colour TV/video lounge, swimming pool, communal bath, kitchen, bbq - single $15, double $20.

Magnetic Island Hostel, 80 Picnic Street, Picnic Bay, ph 785 755 - 6 x 3 bedrooms only - 300m from PO, fans, linen hire, colour TV lounge, 3 baths, kitchens, bbq - $12 per person, 7th night free.

LOCAL TRANSPORT

Magnetic Island Bus Service, 44 Mandalay Avenue, Nelly Bay, ph (077) 785 130, has a service that meets every ferry every day of the year, and goes on an Explorer-type trip around the island, calling at all the attractions and all accommodation outlets. Fares are $6 adult, $3 child, $15 family for the all-day Explorer Day Pass.

Magnetic Island All White Taxi, 6 Lilac Street, Picnic Bay, ph (077) 785 484, has three cabs operating 18 hours per day, seven days per week. Pick up and wheelchair facilities, bookings, ferry connections, tours and sightseeing in air conditioned cars with fares regulated by Queensland Transport.

Holiday Moke Hire, The Jetty Cafe, Picnic Bay Mall, ph (077) 785 703, have Mini Mokes, Suzuki Sierras, 5 and 8 seater vans and Pulsar 5 door hatch. Rates include insurance and fuel. Open daily, 9am-5pm, after hours by arrangement - Mokes $26 + 30c/km over 25 years, $29 + 30c/km 21-24 years (reduced rates 5 days or more).

Magnetic Island Rent A Moke, Shop 4, The Esplanade, Picnic Bay, ph (077) 785 377 - Moke, Mazda 121 and Suzuki Sierras - packages available. Rates include fuel and insurance, 24 hour hire, reduced rates for 5, 7 and 14 days. Open 7 days - day hire $27 + 30c/km Moke; $45 + 30c/km Mazda; $30 + 30c/km Suzuki Sierra.

Road Runner & Scooter Hire, Shop 7, The Esplanade, Picnic Bay, ph (077) 785 222 - single seat 50cc mopeds (scooter) hire.

Open 7 days. Rates include helmet and free kilometres. Half day and hourly rates available - $25 per day.

EATING OUT

The Arcadia Hotel Resort has a few eateries, ranging from a poolside snack bar to the expensive *Gatsby's Restaurant*.

There are other restaurants and cafes at Arcadia and a few at Picnic Bay, Nelly Bay and Horseshoe Bay. Alternatively there is a small shopping centre in Arcadia and a general store at Horseshoe Bay where you can get supplies and cook for yourself.

SIGHTSEEING

Picnic Bay

This is where the ferry docks, and where many people choose to stay. A lookout above the town offers some good views, and to the west is Cockle Bay and the wreck of the *City of Adelaide*, which went aground in 1916. To the east is Rocky Bay, and a lovely secluded beach.

Nelly Bay

Continuing in an easterly direction the next stop is Nelly Bay, home to Shark World, an aquarium complex where feeding times are 11.30am and 2pm. Admission to this attraction is a pricey $5.

The beach near the aquarium has shade and barbecue facilities, and at low tide the reef is visible. Some pioneer graves are found at the end of Nelly Bay, but the ruins that are visible are not from old buildings but from a proposed marina that went wrong.

Arcadia

The next bay you come to is Geoffrey Bay, with a 400m low-tide reef walk that begins at the southern end of the beach. There's a signboard that marks the starting point. Also here is the town of Arcadia, where the ferry also docks, and the Arcadia Hotel Resort, presently the only resort on the island. The Resort offers all kinds of entertainment for guests and visitors, but one that is strictly "Queensland" happens every Wednesday - cane toad racing. For the uninitiated, cane toads are repulsive creatures that were imported from Hawaii years and years ago to eat a bug that was causing trouble for sugar cane growers. When in Hawaii the toads loved the bug and couldn't get enough of it; once in Australia they couldn't have cared less about the bug, but found plenty they did like to eat and began to live happy and contented lives which, of course, resulted in more and more cane toads.

Anyway, back to the races. The person in charge of the meeting catches at least twelve toads, paints a different coloured stripe on each of them and auctions them off to the highest bidders in the waiting crowd. The animals are then put into the middle of a circle and the first one to hop over the outside ring is declared the winner, and his "owner" scoops the pool. At a "serious" meeting this can make the owner several hundred dollars richer.

The Arcadia Pottery Gallery is 200m from the hotel at 44 Armand Way (Horseshoe Bay Road), ph (077) 785 600, and it is open daily 9am-4pm. It displays and sells work from dozens of potters and is worth visiting even if you are not intending to buy.

Continuing around the island the next bay is **Arthur Bay**, where there are reef fish caves, then **Florence Bay**, a sheltered shady beach where you can visit "The Forts". These are relics of World War II and consist of a command post, and signal station, gun sites and an ammunition store. The views from here are fantastic.

Then there is **Balding Bay** which can only be reached by walking track or by sea, and around the point is **Horseshoe Bay**, home to the Koala Park Oasis, Horseshoe Bay Lagoon Environmental Park, water birds and a Mango farm. The Koala Park Oasis also has wombats, kangaroos, wallabies, emus and birds, and is open daily 9am-5pm. Admission is $7 adult, $3.50 child.

Further around is **Five Beach Bay**, which is only accessible by boat, and **West Point**, a very secluded area that people say has the best sunsets ever seen.

SPORT

There is a golf course at Picnic Bay and horse riding at Horseshoe Bay - *Blueys Horseshoe Ranch Trail Rides*, 38 Gifford Street, ph (077) 785 109, $30 for 2 hour bush and beach ride, $45 for half-day bush and beach + morning tea. Blueys is open daily 7am-7pm.

Magnetic Attractions Watersports, at the Boat Ramp, Horseshoe Bay, ph (077) 785 169, offer beach hire, as follows: paraflying ($30), water skiing ($20), jet skiing ($20), catamaran ($20), aqua bike ($6-10), boats and motors (from $20), free stinger suits, waverunners. Open daily, weather permitting.

Nelly Bay Sail Hire, Nelly Bay Beach next to Sharkworld), ph (077) 785 760, have catamaran hire, with free tuition, for $15 per hour, weather and tides permitting.

Pleasure Divers, Arcadia Resort Shopping Centre, Arcadia Bay, ph (077) 785 788, is a dive shop and dive school with scuba hire, snorkel hire, reef and island bookings, adventure bookings and Saturday night dives - from $199 open Water PADI. Open daily 9am-4.30pm.

TOURS

Explorer Leisure Tours, 44 Mandalay Avenue, Nelly Bay, ph (077) 785 130, offer fully conducted tours to all major places of interest, including Radical Bay - $7 adult, $3.50 child, $17.50 family.

Magnetic Tours, 66 Henry Lawson Drive, Horseshoe Bay, ph (077) 785 417, off a bus tour of Magnetic Island including beaches, bay lookouts, local history with full commentary - $5.50 adult, $2.75 child.

Worripa Day Sail, Horseshoe Bay, ph (077) 785 937, have a day sail to some Magnetic Island bays, seafood bbq lunch, snorkelling, fishing, tunnel diving, boom netting, morning/afternoon tea, free courtesy coach, daily 10am-4.30pm - $40 adult, $20 child, $105 family.

ORPHEUS ISLAND

Orpheus Island has an area of 14 sq km and is the second largest in the Palm Island group. There are ten main islands in the group, but eight of them are Aboriginal reservations and permission must be obtained to visit. Orpheus is national park and Pelorus, the other island not part of the reserve, is Crown Land.

Named, in 1887, after the HMS *Orpheus*, the largest warship in Australia when it sank off New Zealand in 1863 with the loss of 188 lives, the island is 80km north of Townsville, and roughly 20km off Lucinda Point near Ingham. Orpheus is long and narrow and its fringing reef is probably the best of all the resort islands. It is heavily wooded and is home to a large population of wild goats. The goats were introduced many years ago as food for people who might be shipwrecked on the island, but they have obviously not been needed and have multiplied to the point where they are causing some problems.

There are a few beaches on the island, although some, eg Hazard Bay and Pioneer Bay, are only suitable for swimming at high tide. When the tide is out they become wading pools. Mangrove Bay and Yankee Bay are good places to swim at low tide.

As far as bush walks are concerned, there is a shortage of them on this island. Up to Fig Tree Hill is one, and from Hazard Bay through a forest to Picnic Bay is another.

There is a Marine Research Station, part of James Cook University, at Little Pioneer Bay, and it is engaged in breeding clams, both giant and other species, and transplanting them to other reefs where there is a shortage of them through overgathering. It is possible to visit the station, but prior arrangements should be made by contacting the station manager, ph (077) 777 336.

The zoning for most of the water around Orpheus is Marine National Park B, although part of the south-west coast is zoned "A". So limited line fishing is allowed in the "A" part, but collecting shells or coral is strictly forbidden.

HOW TO GET THERE

By Air

The Resort arranges to fly guests by seaplane from either Townsville or Cairns, and return fares are: from Townsville $270 return; from Cairns $420 return. The island also has a helipad, but if you wish to charter a helicopter for the trip arrangements must be made through the resort management, ph (077) 777 377.

By Sea

Lucinda Reef & Island Charter Service, ph (077) 778 220, have an "on demand" service from Dungeness, Lucinda, on a 40' flybridge cruiser. The return fare is $120 per person. To get to Lucinda, turn off the Bruce Highway at Ingham.

ACCOMMODATION

The **Resort** has 23 studio units that are rated 3-star.

Resort facilities are: restaurant, cocktail bar, lounge, bbq area, entertainment, games room, tour desk, recreation room, 2 swimming pools, spa, boutique, tennis court, waterskiing, windsurfers, catamarans, snorkelling, paddleboards, boat charter, SCUBA diving, canoes, picnic lunches and laundry.

Room facilities are: private bathrooms, hairdryer, bathrobes, tea/coffee making facilities, refrigerator, mini bar, ceiling fans, radio/music, air-conditioning, non-smoking rooms, iron, daily cleaning service.

Tariff for one night per person/twin share is $380; for five nights it is $1807, and $362 for each additional night. These rates include all meals, snacks and most activities. Not included are those activities that require power. Note that there is no tariff for children: that is because people under 15 years of age are not accepted at the Resort. Day trippers are not allowed in either. Also note that there is no TV on the island.

Reservations can be made through any travel agent or Qantas Travel Centres throughout the world, or through the Resort. The postal address is Orpheus Island Resort, Private Mail Bag 15, Townsville, Qld, 4810, and their telephone number for overseas callers is + 61 77 777 377, for calls from within Australia the toll free number is (008) 077 167.

Credit cards accepted: American Express, Bankcard, MasterCard, Diners Club, Visa.

Camping

Camp sites are found at Pioneer Bay and Yankee Bay. They are patrolled, and have picnic tables, toilets and drinking water. Further information and booking centres: Great Barrier Reef Wonderland, Flinders Street East, Townsville, 4810, ph (077) 212 399; 11 Lannercost Street (PO Box 1293), Ingham 4850, ph (077) 761 700. Campers cannot buy meals at the Resort, and fires are not permitted on the island, so if intending to camp bring all your provisions and a fuel stove.

DIVING

As mentioned previously, Orpheus has some of the best fringing reef of all the islands, and good reefs are also found off Pelorus Island to the north and Fantome Island to the south. The Resort dive shop offers local dives and diving courses, but remember that these activities are definitely not included in the Resort tariff.

Pioneer Bay

THE CASSOWARY COAST

The Cassowary Coast incorporates the towns of Cardwell, Tully and Mission Beach, and is the stepping off point for the great Hinchinbrook Channel, that is renowned for its barramundi, mangrove jack and many other table fish.

Ferries to Hinchinbrook Island National Park leave from Cardwell, and the town also offers estuary and reef fishing trips. You can also organise fully guided or self drive tours through world heritage forests, and scenic attractions such as the beautiful Murray Falls and the wild Blencoe Falls.

Tully is a sugar town that nestles at the foot of the mountain range. Quite close is the Tully River, famous for its white water rapids, and there are many operators in town that are ready to take you white water rafting.

Mission Beach has a cassowary reserve, great sandy beaches, and a water taxi service to nearby Dunk Island.

HOW TO GET THERE

Tully is on the Bruce Highway 106km north of Ingham; 222km north of Townsville; 152km south of Cairns. Cardwell is also on the Bruce Highway, about half-way between Tully and Ingham. Mission Beach is on a loop road that branches off the Bruce Highway at Ingham.

TOURIST INFORMATION

Cardwell Tourist Association (PO Box 14, Cardwell), ph (070) 668 648, can be found at the Kookaburra Holiday Park, 175 Bruce Highway.

Tully Information Office is on the western side of the Bruce Highway, ph (070) 682 288, and it is open Mon-Fri 9am-5pm,

Sat-Sun 9am-noon, although it may not be open on the weekends during the off season.

Mission Beach Information Office is at the northern end of Porters Promenade, ph (070) 687 099, and is open daily 9am-5pm.

ACCOMMODATION

Following is a selection of accommodation in the three towns, with prices for a double room per night, which should be used as a guide only. The telephone area code is 070.

Cardwell

Lyndoch Motor Inn, 215 Victoria Street, ph 668 500 - 19 rooms, licensed restaurant, swimming pool, bbq, facilities for the disabled - $40-45

Sunrise Village, 43A Marine Parade, ph 668 550 - 40 rooms, licensed restaurant, swimming pool, spa, bbq, facilities for the disabled - $35-45.

Aquarius Units, 25 Victoria Street, ph 668 755 - 6 units, swimming pool, spa, kitchen facilities, bbq, some facilities for disabled - $45-55.

Cardwell Beachfront, 1 Scott Street, ph 668 776 - 5 units, swimming pool, bbq - $45.

Island Lure Flats, 17 Victoria Street, ph 668 787 - 4 units, swimming pool, kitchen facilities, bbq - $30.

Kookaburra Holiday Park, 175 Bruce Highway, ph 668 648 - 1km from town, kiosk, bbq, swimming pool, sporting equipment - cabins $32; tent sites $10; van sites $12; on-site vans $26.

Banfield, 107 Roma Street, ph 668 689 - 400m from PO and shops - tent sites $9; van sites $10; on-site vans $15.

Meunga Creek Caravan Park, Bruce Highway, ph 668 710 - kiosk, bbq - tent sites $8; van sites $10; on-site vans $17.

Pacific Palms Caravan Park, 186 Bruce Highway, ph 668 671 - kiosk, bbq, playground, facilities for the disabled, swimming pool, takeaway food, EFTPOS machine - cabin $30; tent sites $10; van sites $12; on-site vans $27.

Hinchinbrook Hostel, 175 Bruce Highway, ph 668 648 - 4

dormitories, 15 beds, 3 double rooms, communal facilities, swimming pool, shop - single $26, twin $26, bunkhouse $12 per person.

Tully

Mons Mari Motel, Bruce Highway, ph 682 233 - 9 units, 9-hole golf course, facilities for the disabled, bbq - $47.

Googarra Beach Caravan Park, Hull Heads, ph 669 325 - kiosk/general store, bbq, facilities for the disabled, swimming pool, playground - cabins $35; tent sites $7; van sites $11; on-site vans $85 per week.

Island Coast Van Park, Tully Heads Beach, Tully Heads, ph 669 260 - beachfront, kiosk, bbq, facilities for the disabled, swimming pool - cabins $35; tent sites $12; van sites $12; on-site vans $25.

Tully Caravan Park, Murray Street, ph 682 055 - 500m from town centre, kiosk, bbq - cabins $30; tent sites $8; van sites $10; on-site vans $55-80 per week.

Mission Beach

The Point Resort, Mitchell Street, South Mission Beach, ph 688 154 - 28 rooms, licensed restaurant, swimming pool, spa, shop sport facilities - $138.

Castaways Beach Resort, Seaview Street, ph 687 444 - 54 rooms, licensed restaurant, facilities for the disabled, bbq, shop, swimming pool, spa - $90.

Mission Beach Resort, Wongaling Beach Road, ph 688 288 - 76 rooms, licensed restaurant, swimming pool, spa, sport facilities, facilities for the disabled - $85.

Anchor In, 108 Kennedy Esplanade, South Mission Beach, ph 831 200 - 4 units, swimming pool, full kitchen, tea/coffee making, bbq, shop, linen hire - $50-65.

Lugger Bay Rainforest Apartments, 18 Explorers Drive, South Mission Beach, ph 688 400 - 6 units, swimming pool, spa, licensed restaurant nearby - from $175 for 2.

Ceud Mile Failte, 23 Porter Promenade, ph 687 144 - 4 units, full kitchen, tea/coffee making, bbq, swimming pool, linen for hire - $55.

Golden Sands Units, South Mission Beach, ph 681 013 - 7 units, full kitchen, tea/coffee making, bbq, swimming pool - $50-70.

Beachcomber Coconut Village, Kennedy Esplanade, South Mission Beach, ph 688 129 - kiosk, half tennis court, bbq, facilities for the disabled, playground, swimming pool, boat hire - cabins $31-44; tent sites $11.50; van sites $13.50; camp-o-tel $18.

Dunk Island View Park, 175 Reid Road, ph 688 248 - 4km from town, kiosk, bbq, playground, swimming pool, table tennis - cabins $42; tent sites $10.50; van sites $12.50; on-site vans $27.

Mission Beach Caravan Park, Porters Promenade, ph 611 222 - playground, kiosk, swimming pool - tent sites $5; van sites $9.

Scottys Beach House, 167 Reid Road, ph 688 676 - 5km from PO, swimming pool, communal bath, kitchen, laundry, bbq - double $27; bunkhouse $12; garden rooms (with air condition and ensuite) $35.

Mission Beach Backpackers, 28 Wongaling Beach Road, ph 688 317 - 48 beds, 3km from PO, swimming pool, sport facilities, spa, communal bath, kitchen, laundry, bike hire - double $28-33; bunkhouse $12.

Treehouse Hostel, Frizelle Road, ph 687 137 - 7km from town, free linen, swimming pool, communal bath, kitchen, laundry, bbq, shop - $13; camping sites $9 per person.

SIGHTSEEING

CARDWELL is a fishing village situated between the mountains and the sea. It is in the middle of a natural wonderland, with world heritage rainforests, waterfalls, swimming holes, wilderness tracks, white water rafting, canoeing, crabbing, fishing and prawning. The Cardwell lookout offers panoramic coastal views and there are very scenic drives to Murray Falls, Blencoe Falls, the Edmund Kennedy National Park, Dalrymple's Gap Track and Cardwell Forest.

On the Bruce Highway there is the *Shiralee Camel Farm*, ph (070) 668 137, with a museum and the chance to ride a camel.

Cardwell is also the gateway to Hinchinbrook Island, the world's largest Island National Park.

Tours

Hinchinbrook Adventures, 135 Victoria Street, Cardwell, ph (070) 668 270, offer:

Garden or Goold Island - high speed catamaran transfer, swimming, fishing - 7 hours - $35 adult, $18 child - daily 9.30am.

Camper Transfers - high speed catamaran transfers to Ramsay Bay, Macushla, Garden and Goold Islands - $40 return adult, $20 return child - daily - 9.30am.

Reef Fishing - Kennedy shoals and Otter Reef with experienced skipper and crew - bait, ice, lines and tackle included - $100 - Sat-Sun - 6am.

Ramsay Bay - high speed catamaran transfer, mangrove tour, swimming beach, fossilised crabs, scenery - 7 hours - $40 adult, $20 child, $100 family - Wed, Fri Sun - 9.30am.

Macushla - high speed catamaran transfer, NP self-guided rainforest walk (5km), ocean beach, optional resort lunch - 7 hours - $35 adult, $18 child, $95 family - daily - 9.30am.

Cape Richards/Resort - high speed catamaran transfer, swim on ocean beach, optional lunch at resort ($25) - 7 hours - $40 adult, $20 child, $100 family - daily - 9.30am.

Brook Island - reef snorkelling, clear reef 40 mins from Cardwell - all equipment included + morning tea (lunch extra) - 7 hours - $40 adult, $12.50 child, $100 family - Sat - 9.30am (weather permitting).

Hinchinbrook Island Cruises, Bruce Highway (next to Ampol Service Station), Cardwell, ph (070) 668 539, offer:

Ramsay Bay Everglades Cruise - 6km mangrove everglades, 9km beach for swimming, fossilised crabs - 7 1/2 hours - $43 adult, $20 child (11-14), $5 child (4-10), $100 family - Mon, Tues, Thurs - 9am.

Macushla Walk - 5km walk through rainforest, swimming, optional lunch at Hinchinbrook Resort - $35 adult, $16 child (11-14), $5 child (4-10) - Mon,Tues, Thurs, Fri, Sat - 9am.

Brook Island Reef Cruise - 3 hours snorkelling, swimming, lunch optional extra - 7 1/2 hours total - $43 adult, $20 child (11-14), $5 child (4-10), $100 family - Sun, Wed - 9am.

Cape Richards/Resort - lazy day on beach, option as day guest at resort, bush walk, cruise - 7 1/2 hours - $35 adult, $16 child (11-14), $5 child (4-10), $90 family - daily - 9am.

Camper Transfers/Ramsay Bay - east coast trail, 35km walk to George Point at south end - 3 nights 4 days at own pace - $30 on $40 return - daily - 9am.

Camper Transfers/Macushla - 20km walk track, 2 beaches for swimming, water tank, shelter shed, bush toilet - $40 adult, $20 child - daily - 9am.

Cardwell Day Tours, PO Box 100, Cardwell, ph (070) 668 741, offer:

Paronella Park, via Licuala State Forest Park, Mission Beach, coastal rainforest, cane fields, Paronella ruins - full day - $40 adult6, $20 child - BYO lunch - 9am.

World Heritage Safari - visit spectacular Blencoe Falls, lunch by Blencoe Creek, educational tour of world heritage forests - 9 hours - $40 adult, $20 child - BYO lunch - 8am.

Forest & Falls Explorer - explore the forest drive, creeks, swim holes and water falls - $35 adult, $18 child - BYO lunch - 9am.

Cardwell Fishing Safari, Meunga Creek Boat Ramp Road, Cardwell, ph (070) 668 064, offer personalised small parties - all bait, tackle and lures supplied - catch crab, barramundi, snap a croc, all in calm estuaries - full day - $35 per person - BYO lunch.

Hinchinbrook Sail Safaris, Lot 1, Stoney Creek Road, Cardwell,

Sugar cane fire, Cassowary Coast region.

ph (070) 668 143, offer 3 day tour of Hinchinbrook and surrounding islands, including trekking, swimming, snorkelling, accommodation, food and pick-up - $145 adult, $100 child (under 10) - Mon, Thurs - 8am. They also have a day sail that includes lunch and pick-up for an 8am departure - $48 adult, $28 child (under 10).

TULLY is first and foremost a sugar town, but it should also be noted that it has the highest annual rainfall in Australia (along with Innisfail) of around 3700mm. There is a definite Wet Season which begins in December and peaks in March. During this period it can rain every day, and sometimes all day. People intending to spend their holiday on either Dunk or Bedarra Islands should bear this fact in mind. Tropical Islands become somewhat less than paradise when the rain just doesn't stop.

Tours
One hour tours of the *Sugar Mill* can be arranged through the information centre, ph (070) 682 288 - $5 per person, $12 family - Mon-Fri at 10am.

Raging Thunder, 111 Spence Street, Cairns, ph (070) 311 466, offer rafting on the Tully River. An all day tour includes lunch, dinner and 5 hours of action - $112 - Tues, Thurs, Sat, Sun - pick-up at local accommodation.

The information office will be able to advise on other river trips.

Hinchinbrook Fish 'N Float Safari, PO Box 340, Tully, ph (070) 686 201, offer estuary fishing in the Hinchinbrook Channel and raft fishing in the Tully River - prices include pick-up and deliver in the Tully region, bait and tackle - $230 for 2 person boat Estuary, $80 per person in 4 person boat River.

MISSION BEACH has a population of 660, and is set on a stretch of 14km of coastline that includes Garners Beach, Bingil Bay, Narragon Beach, Clump Point and Wongaling Beach. There is a daily water taxi service from Mission to nearby Dunk Island, and many visitors choose to stay on the mainland and visit the islands, rather than pay resort prices.

The town is named after the Aboriginal Mission that was set up in 1912 at South Mission Beach, but the first settlers were the Cutten brothers who landed to the north at Bingil Bay in 1882 and founded a farming dynasty. They introduced pineapple growing to this part of Queensland and founded tea and coffee plantations. In 1918 the "cyclone of the century" levelled the settlements and farms in the district.

Nowadays the main industries are banana and sugar-cane growing, and tourism.

Tours

Dunk Island Ferry & Cruises, Clump Point Jetty, Mission Beach, ph (070) 687 211, offer:

Dunk Island Return - full commentary, licensed bar, sundeck or undercover - $20 adult, $10 child - daily - 8.55am and 10.30am.

Dunk Island Return with BBQ Lunch - full commentary, view Family Islands, steak/seafood & salads lunch - $28 adult, $18 child - daily - 8.55am and 10.30am.

Three in One Special - Dunk Island return, bbq lunch, Bedarra Island cruise, 1 1/2 hours through Family Isles, boom netting, tropical fruit - $41 adult, $20.50 child - daily - 8.55am and 10.30am.

Evening Cruises - dancing, bar, - POA.

MV Quick Cat, Clump Point, Mission Beach, ph (070) 687 289, offer:

Dunk Island - visit resort, Mt Kootaloo, Banfield's grave, swinging bridge - $19 adult, $9.50 child, $49 family - daily - 10.15am, return 5.15pm.

Great Barrier Reef - Beaver reef and cay, snorkel, swim, option scuba, includes lunch and far facilities, Dunk Island afternoon visit - 7hours-$94 adult, $47 child, $235 family -daily- 10.15am.

Uninhabited Island Cruise - includes lunch - $38 adult, $19 child, $99 family.

Dowd's Coaches & Water Taxi, Banfield Parade, Wongaling Beach, ph (070) 688 310, run a Mission Beach to Dunk Island water taxi with seven trips daily, 10 minutes each way. The taxi departs from Wongaling Beach and return fares are $18 adult, $9 child - 8am-5.30pm daily.

Friendship Cruises, Clump Point Jetty, Mission Beach, ph (070) 687 262, offer;

Great Barrier Reef - Beaver or Taylor Reef, snorkel, glass bottom boat, tame fish, morning/afternoon tea, BYO lunch - all equipment supplied - $49 adult, $24.50 child - scuba: $84 certified, $99 resort (boat fare included - daily - 8.30am.

Great Barrier Reef Dive Inn, Shop 4, The Hub Shopping Centre, Mission Beach, ph (070) 687 294, offer scuba diving, retail, courses, tuition, equipment sales and service, dive trips, hire equipment - fast vessel to various reefs and 24 different dive sites - $89 certified divers, $100 resort divers, all equipment supplied - 7 days - good rates for diving clubs.

Mission Beach/Dunk Island Water Taxi, 120 Kennedy Esplanade, South Mission Beach, ph (070) 688 333, have daily trips to Dunk Island taking approximately 10 minutes - free time Dunk Island, return at leisure - $18 adult return, $9 child.

Mission Beach Rainforest Treks, Frizelle Road, Mission Beach, ph (070) 687 137, offer:

Rainforest Nightwalk - Lacey Creek area, includes pick-up, torches, guided tour, forestry permits - 3 hours - $12 adult, $12 child - on demand - 7.40pm.

Rainforest Morning Walk - Lacey Creek area, includes pick-up, binoculars, guided tour, morning tea, permit - $18 adult, $18 child - 4 hours - on demand - 6am.

Cassowary Day Trek - 8km trek through unopened rainforest inhabited by cassowaries, includes meal and pick-up - $40 adult - on demand - 8.30am.

White Water Day Trek - trail along rainforest stream, with rapids and waterfalls, to swimming hole, includes pick-up and meal - $50 adult - on demand - 8.30am.

MV Cloud 9, PO Box 119, Mission Beach 4854, ph (070) 688 339 - charter game fishing boat - reef fishing and snorkelling on share basis. Dive charters by arrangement, 7 days per week - Hinchinbrook Island cruises - min6, max 12 on share basis - $99 per person, including lunch.

HINCHINBROOK ISLAND

Hinchinbrook is the world's largest island national park, with over 45,000ha (393 sq km) of tropical rainforests, mountains, gorges, valleys, waterfalls and sandy beaches.

It is separated from the mainland by Hinchinbrook Channel, a narrow mangrove-fringed strip of water that is very deep. From further out at sea, the channel cannot be seen, and in fact, when Captain Cook sailed past he did not record the presence of an island.

Aborigines lived on the island and remains of their fish traps can be seen near the Scraggy Point camp site.

The best walk on any of the Great Barrier Reef islands is the three to four day walk along the eastern side of Hinchinbrook, but it is strongly recommended that information be obtained from QNP&WS before setting out. They have an office on the Bruce Highway at Cardwell and can advise on facilities on the island, give tips for climbing the mountains and protecting your supplies from the local wildlife, and issue permits for camping.

Remember that marine stingers may be around in the October-May period, and that crocodiles may be found in channel waters and estuaries.

HOW TO GET THERE

See the section on Tours from Cardwell. These same boats can be used to transfer people to Hinchinbrook.

ACCOMMODATION

The **Resort** on Hinchinbrook is on Cape Richards at the north of the island. Its maximum capacity is 50 guests, housed in 7 cabins and 15 treehouses, all with their own bathrooms, tea/coffee making facilities and a refrigerator. The cabins have two bedrooms, and the newer treehouses have one or two. There is no TV or radio on the island, and only one telephone.

There is a restaurant, a bar, a barbecue near the swimming pool, canoes, snorkelling gear, surf skis, fishing equipment, shop and a lending library. There is almost nothing in the way of night life, and even during the day there is not much in the way of organised activity. Hinchinbrook is a real "get away from it all" place.

Tariff for one night is:

Cabins - $200 single, $380 double, $65 child.

Treehouses - $290 single, $530 double, $90 child.

These rates include all meals and use of most of the equipment (except those requiring power).

Hinchinbrook Resort closes for about two months every year - from late January until Easter.

Camping

Macushla Camping Area - patrols, picnic tables, shelter shed, toilets, fires prohibited - $5 /site/night ($30/site/week) for up to six people.

The Haven (Scraggy Point) Camping Area - toilets, fires prohibited - $2/site/night ($12/site/week) for up to six people.

Zoe Bay Camping Area - toilets, fires prohibited - $2/site/night ($12/site/week) for up to six people.

Bush Camping - fires prohibited - $2/site/night ($12/site/week) for up to six people.

BEDARRA ISLAND

Part of the Family Group of Islands, Bedarra lies about 6km south of Dunk Island and about 5km offshore. It is privately owned and is shown on marine charts as Richards Island.

Bedarra has an area of one sq km, and is a rainforest with natural springs and plenty of water. It has some very good sandy beaches. Note that it has a very definite Wet Season from December to the end of March, when it can rain every day and sometimes all day.

Originally occupied by Aboriginals, the island was purchased by Captain Henry Allason from the Queensland Land Department for £20, and they threw in Timana Island for good luck. He sold Bedarra to Ivan Menzies, in the 1920s, for £500, and it then passed through several pairs of hands until it reached Dick Greatrix and Pierre Huret, who established gardens at the sandspit end, at what is now the Hideaway Resort. A section of the island had been sold to Australian artist Noel Wood in 1936, and another artist John Busst, leased the south-east corner. His home became the Plantation Resort (Bedarra Bay), and in 1947, Geatrix and Huret sold out to him. The island was passed around a few times more before TAA bought the northern part in 1980, and the southern part in 1981. TAA was to become Australian Airlines, and is now part of Qantas.

Both resorts were completely rebuilt, and Bedarra Bay reopened in 1986, but the Hideaway has yet to reopen. The prediction is June or December 1996, but it seems that nobody knows for sure. There is a walking track from Bedarra Bay to the Hideaway, in fact, it is the only walking track on the island.

HOW TO GET THERE

Bedarra Island is reached via Dunk Island. The boat connects with flights to/from dunk and the water taxis between Dunk and the mainland.

ACCOMMODATION

Bedarra Bay Resort is on the eastern side of the island. It has 16 villas that are rated 5-star.

Resort facilities are: restaurant, cocktail lounge, swimming pool, spa, floodlit tennis court, laundry service, dinghies with outboards, sailboarding, snorkelling, fishing equipment,

EFTPOS.

Villa facilities are: bathroom with bath, hair dryer and bath robes, queen size beds, refrigerator, mini bar, air-conditioning, ceiling fans, radio, telephone IDD/STD, daily cleaning service, beach towels, writing desk, separate living area, colour TV, video cassette recorder, private balcony.

Tariff for one night per person/twin share is $530, which includes accommodation, all meals, drinks (including alcohol) and most activities.

Not included in the tariff are: Great Barrier Reef trips, boutique/shop, float plains, game fishing charters, hair salon (available on Dunk Island), private boat charters, sailing charters.

Note that children under 15 years are not accepted at the Resort, and that maximum villa occupancy is 3 persons.

Reservations can be made through any travel agent, Australian Resorts, ph 008 812 525 (7 days), from overseas ph (+ 61 7) 360 2444, or through any Qantas office. The Resort address is Bedarra Bay Resort, Bedarra Island, via Townsville, 4810, ph (070) 688 233), fax (070) 688 215.

Credit cards accepted: Visa, MasterCard, Bank-card, Diners Club, American Express, JCB.

Typical reef scenery

TOWNSVILLE

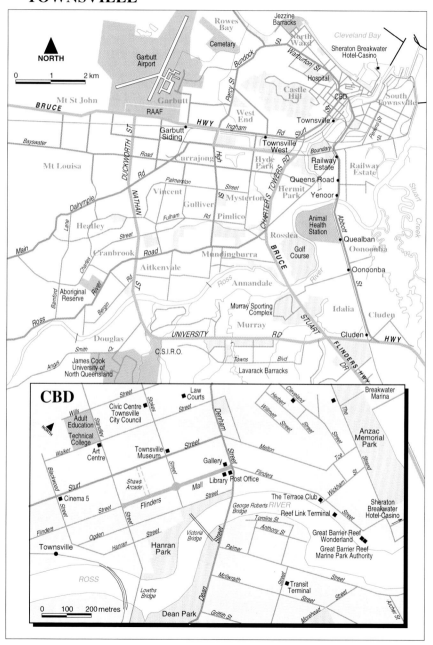

TOWNSVILLE to CAIRNS

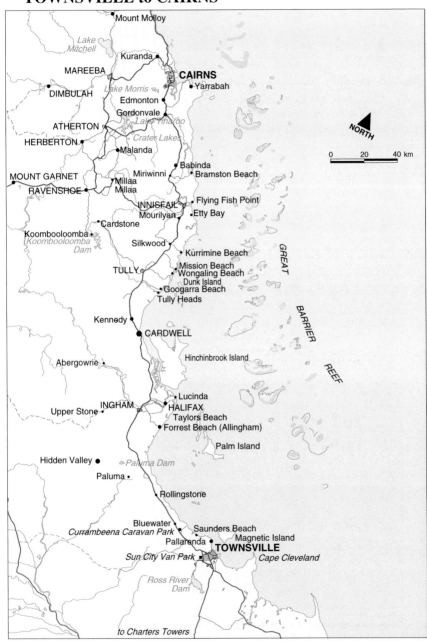

DUNK ISLAND

Dunk Island is also part of the Family group of islands, and its Aboriginal name is Coonanglebah which means "isle of peace and plenty". Captain Cook named it Dunk after Lord Montague Dunk, the Earl of Sandwich, who was the First Lord of the Admiralty at the time.

It is the largest island in the group and is sometimes called the Father of the Family Group (Bedarra is the Mother). The island's area is 10 sq km, but 7.3 sq km is national park. The Wet Season, when it is best not to visit, lasts from December to the end of March.

Cook recorded that Aborigines on these islands stood in groups and watched the *Endeavour* sail past, but they have long gone from the area. The earliest long term European resident was E.J. Banfield, who lived there from 1897 to 1923. He was a journalist on *The Townsville Daily Bulletin* when his doctor told him to slow down or face the consequences. So he and his wife decided to get back to nature and live on Dunk, where they were apparently very happy. When he wasn't tending his garden, Banfield wrote articles for his old newspaper, or worked on his books - *Confessions of a Beachcomber* (1908), *My Tropic Isle* (1911), *Tropic Days* (1918) and *Last Leaves from Dunk Island* (1925), the last published after his death.

The Banfields' house became part of a small resort that was opened in 1934 by Spenser Hopkins, a friend of theirs, but a year later that part of the island was sold with Hopkins only keeping the section where the Artists' Colony is today.

During the second world war a radar station was set up on Mt Kootaloo and proved its worth during the Battle of the Coral Sea. Its remains can still be seen.

The resort changed hands a few times until 1978 when TAA became sole owner, so Qantas, the present owner, acquired Dunk with its takeover of Australian Airlines (formerly TAA).

Dunk is very much a family resort and it has some good high tide beaches, but at low tide they are too shallow and have a lot of weed. The island doesn't seem to have a problem with box jellyfish, but it is wise to keep an eye out during the November-March period.

There are 13km of walking tracks, and the 10km walk around the island rates amongst the best on any of the Barrier Reef islands.

HOW TO GET THERE

By Air

Sunstate Airlines have flights to Dunk from Townsville and Cairns and both flights take 45 minutes.

By Sea

Water taxis from Mission Beach to Dunk are operated by *Dowd's Coaches & Water Taxi*, ph (070) 688 310, and *Mission Beach/Dunk Island Water Taxi*, ph (070) 688 333. See Mission Beach Tours section for more information.

ACCOMMODATION

The **Resort** accommodation consists of 141 rooms divided into four categories: Bayview Villa (4-star); Beachfront Unit (3 1/2-star); Garden Cabana Unit (3-star); and Banfield Unit (3-star).

Resort facilities are: live entertainment, restaurant, brasserie, cocktail bar, games room, two swimming pools, spa, tennis courts, laundry/ironing, Kids Club, babysitting, snorkelling, catamaran sailing, parasailing, sailboarding, fishing, cricket, waterskiing, horse riding, golf, archery, tube rides, clay shooting, squash, Barrier Reef cruises and air tours, cruising and coral viewing, SCUBA diving, tandem sky-diving, beach volleyball, EFTPOS.

Unit facilities are: tea/coffee making facilities, refrigerator, colour TV, in-house movies, IDD/STD telephone, radio, air-conditioning, ceiling fans, daily cleaning service, balcony or verandah, inter-connecting rooms.

Tariffs for one night per person/twin share are:

Banfield - $161 (child 3-14 sharing with 2 adults - free)

Garden Cabana - $185 (child - as above)

Beachfront - $238 (child - as above)

Bayview - $248 (child - as above).

The above rates are room only, but there is a meal option, with costs for one night as follows:

Breakfast - $22 adult, $11 child

Breakfast and Dinner - $54 adult, $27 child

Full Board - $70 adult, $38 child.

Additional to the tariffs are: Artists' Colony visits, clay target shooting, game fishing, glass bottom boat tours, golf clinics, horse riding, massage therapist, nature walks and rainforest tours, outboard dinghies, reef cruises, scuba diving and lessons - resort and accredited courses and dive trips to the Great Barrier Reef, sunset cruises, tandem skydiving, tennis clinics, waterskiing.

Reservations can be made through Australian Resorts, ph 008 812 525 (7 days), from overseas ph (+ 61 7) 360 2444, through any Qantas office, or any travel agent. The Resort address is Dunk Island Resort, Dunk Island, via Townsville, 4810, ph (070) 688 199, fax (070) 688528.

Credit cards accepted: Visa, MasterCard, Bankcard, Diners Club, American Express, JCB.

Camping

Camping is permitted on the Foreshore reserve, and information and bookings can be obtained from Rainforest and Reef Centre, Bruce Highway (PO Box 74) Cardwell, 4816, ph (070) 668 601. Fees are $5/site/night ($30/site/week) for up to six people.

Facilities are: picnic tables, toilets, drinking water and showers. No fires are permitted.

Campers and day trippers are welcome to hire the Resort's equipment.

Artists' Colony

Situated just beyond the Resort garden, the colony's longest term resident is former Olympic wrestler Bruce Arthur, who produces large and beautiful tapestries. He and his cohorts lease the land, and have open house on Tuesday and Friday morning ($4 entry) when they chat about the island and their projects, and present their work for sale.

DIVING

The Great Barrier Reef is an hour away by *Quickcat*, the high-speed catamaran, and there are four reefs to dive: Beaver, Farquharson, Yamacutta and Potter. They have some of the best coral and marine life on the Reef, and feature feeding stations, coral walls, caves, caverns and gardens. Trips to Beaver Reef include glass bottom boat, semi-submersible rides, lunch and onboard dive instruction.

All the diving needs on Dunk are catered for by very experienced instructors. Training is available to international levels (PADI & NAUI) in a variety of courses from beginners to most experienced, including: Open Water Course, Advanced Rescue, Divemaster and specialist courses like night diving. Only the very latest equipment is available for hire at reasonable rates.

THE TROPICAL NORTH

F ar North Queensland (the Tropical North) extends from Cardwell in the south to the Torres Strait in the north, and west across the Gulf of Carpentaria to the Northern Territory border, an area of 377,796 sq km, which is almost twice the size of the state of Victoria. Cairns, its major city and service, administration, distribution and manufacturing centre, has recorded the second highest percentage of population growth of any Australian city since 1979.

CAIRNS

Cairns, in the heart of the tropical wonderland, is an international tourist mecca. It is a modern, colourful city situated on the shores of a natural harbour, Trinity Inlet, with a magnificent backdrop of rugged mountains covered with thick tropical rainforest.

The major glamour activity in Cairns is Big Game Fishing, and numerous fish over 450kg are caught each year. The game fishing season starts in early September and continues through to late November, however light game can be caught all year. As well as being a major city for tourists, Cairns is an important centre for the export of sugar and the agricultural products of the Atherton Tablelands. The city was named after William Wellington Cairns, the third Governor of Queensland.

CLIMATE

Average temperatures: January max 32C (90F) - min 24C (75F); July max 25C (77F) - min 16C (61F). The humidity is high in summer, and the best time to visit is from May to October.

The city of Cairns

HOW TO GET THERE

By Air

Cairns International Airport is serviced by several international airlines apart from Qantas, including Canadian Airlines, United Airlines, Air New Zealand and Cathay Pacific.

Ansett Australia and *Qantas* have several flights daily from Brisbane to Cairns, and these connect with flights from other capital cities.

Cairns Domestic and International airports are approximately 6km from the centre of the city. Regular coach services depart from the domestic terminals for the city and the northern beaches, and there is also an inter-terminal coach service.

By Rail

The *Sunlander* arrives in Cairns at 6.10pm on Wed, Fri and Sun. The *Queenslander* and the *Spirit of the Tropics* arrive at 6.10pm on Mondays.

By Bus

Pioneer/Greyhound and McCafferty's operate regular daily express coach services from major southern cities.

By Road

From Brisbane, via the Bruce Highway is 1800km.

TOURIST INFORMATION

The Visitors Information Centre is at the Far North Queensland Promotion Bureau, cnr Aplin and Sheridan Streets, open Mon-Fri 9am-5pm, Sat 9am-4pm, ph (070) 513 588.

ACCOMMODATION

The Cairns area has over 40 motels, as well as hotels, guest houses, holiday apartments and over 20 caravan parks. Prices vary considerably depending on the standard of accommodation and the season. Here is a selection, with prices for a double room per night, which should be used as a guide only. The telephone area code is 070.

Cairns Hilton Hotel, Wharf Street, ph 521 599 - 265 rooms, restaurant, 3 cocktail bars, coffee shop, bbq area, swimming pool, fitness centre, spa, sauna, baby sitting, beauty salon, shopping, tour desk - $108.

Cairns International Hotel, 17 Abbot Street, ph 311 300 - 321 rooms, 2 restaurants, 3 cocktail bars, coffee shop, entertainment, bbq area, 2 swimming pools, fitness centre, spa, sauna, baby sitting, beauty salon, shopping, tour desk - $99.

Radisson Plaza Hotel Pierpoint Road, ph 311 411 - 196 units, 2 restaurants, cocktail bar, coffee shop, 3 swimming pool,s children's pool, fitness centre, spa, sauna, games room, baby sitting, beauty salon, shopping, tour desk - $105-118.

Matson Plaza Hotel, The Esplanade, ph 312 211 - 242 rooms, 2 restaurants, 3 cocktail bars, swimming pool, tennis court, bbq area, fitness centre, spa, sauna, beauty salon, shopping tour desk - $79.

Tradewinds Esplanade Hotel, 137 The Esplanade, ph 521 111 - 241 rooms, brasserie restaurant, restaurant, cocktail bar, entertainment, swimming pool, spa, children's pool, baby sitting, tour desk - $69.

Holiday Inn Cairns, cnr Esplanade & Florence Street, ph 313 757 - 232 rooms, restaurant, cocktail bar, bottle shop, swimming pool, children's pool, spa, baby sitting, shopping, tour desk - $71.

Quality Harbourside Hotel, 209-217 The Esplanade, ph 518 999 - 148 units, restaurant, cocktail bar, swimming pool, children's pool, spa, baby sitting, shopping, tour desk - $67.

Tropic Towers Apartments, 294 Sheridan Street, ph 313 955 - 44 one and two bedroom units, swimming pool and spa, tour desk, bbq - one bedroom $65.00, two bedroom $80.

Palm Royale Hotel, 7-11 Chester Court, ph 322 700 - 134 rooms, restaurant, 2 cocktail bars, coffee shop, swimming pool, spa, tour desk - $63.

Reef Plaza Hotel, cnr Spence & Grafton Streets, ph 411 022 - 98 units, restaurant, cocktail bar, theme bar, bbq area, swimming pool, sauna, baby sitting, beauty salon - $62.

Tuna Towers, 145 The Esplanade, ph 514 688 - 60 units, restaurant, cocktail bar, swimming pool, spa, baby sitting, tour desk - $56.

Country Comfort Outrigger Inn, cnr Abbot & Florence Streets, ph 516 188 - 51 units, restaurant, cocktail bar, bbq area, swimming pool, spa, baby sitting, tour desk - $51.

All Seasons Sunshine Tower, 140 Sheridan Street, ph 515 288 - 61 units, restaurant, cocktail bar, coffee shop, bbq area, 2 swimming pools, spa, baby sitting, tour desk - $50.

High Chaparral Motel, 195-205 Sheridan Street, ph 517 155 - two types of accommodation, motel with kitchenette and self-contained apartments - 2 swimming pools, bbq area, baby sitting service, tour desk - motel $35-41, apartment $38-44.

Caravan Parks

Cairns Coconut Caravan Village, Bruce Highway South (cnr Anderson Road), Woree, ph 546 644 - swimming pool, kiosk, bbq, tennis court, mini golf - en suite sites $20-21, powered sites $16-17, tent sites $14-15; cabins $32-46; units $45-56.

Coles Villa Caravan Park, 28 Pease Street, Manoora, ph 537 133 - kiosk, bbq area, playground, salt water pool - powered sites $15; tent sites $12; units $42-55; cabins $42-55.

Cool Waters Caravan Park, Brinsmead Road, Brinsmead, ph 341 949 - shop, bbq area, rec room, swimming pool - powered sites $14; tent sites $12; cabins $30-50.

Crystal Cascades Holiday Park, Intake Road, Redlynch, ph 391 036 - kiosk, bbq area, salt water pool, spa - powered sites $15; cabins $38-48.

LOCAL TRANSPORT

There are public transport services to all Cairns city areas, suburbs and beaches. Timetables and routes are available at hotels and bus depots.

Cairns City Airporter, ph (070) 359 555, have an airport/city/airport service, and bookings are essential for trips to the airport. They also have vehicles available for charter.

Cairns Trans Buses, ph (070) 352 600, service the suburbs of Edge Hill, Whitfield, Manunda, Westcourt, Earleville, Woree, Bayview, Whiterock, Edmonton, Gordonvale, Yorkeys Knob and Holloways Beach.

Southern Cross Bus Service, ph (070) 551 240, services the suburbs of Stratford, Freshwater, Redlynch and Aeroglen and Machans Beach.

White Car Coaches, ph (070) 519 533, service the Atherton Tablelands and Chillagoe.

West Cairns Bus Service, ph (070) 532 281, services the suburbs of Manunda, North Cairns and Manoora.

The Beach Bus, ph (070) 577411, services the Northern Beaches.

Coral Coaches have daily services between: Cairns, Hartley Creek, Port Douglas, Mossman, Daintree, Cape Tribulation, Bloomfield, Cooktown - Inland and Coast Road. They also have airport transfers to/from: Northern Beaches, Port Douglas, Mossman, Cape Tribulation. Phone Cairns (070) 317 577; Port Douglas (070) 995 351; Mossman (070) 982 600.

Cairns-Karumba Coachlines, ph (070) 518 311, service Cairns across the Gulf to Karumba.

Cape York Coaches, ph (070) 930 176, service Cairns up the Cape to Weipa.

Car Hire

Avis, 135 Lake Street, ph 515 911; Cairns Airport, ph 359 100.

Sugarland Car Rentals, 134 Sheridan Street, Cairns, ph 521 300.

Cairns Rent-A-Car, 147c Lake Street, Cairns, ph 516 077.

Hertz, 147 Lake Street, Cairns, ph 516 399.

Opposite
Skyrail Gondola (Cairns Region).

Mini Car Rentals, 150 Sheridan Street, Cairns, ph (070) 516 288.
Peter's Economy Rent-A-Car, 36 Water Street, Cairns, ph (070) 514 106.
Cassowary Car Hire, 6/43a Grafton St, Cairns, ph (070) 511 188.
Cairns Leisure Wheels, 196a Sheridan Street, Cairns, ph (070) 518 988.
Reef Rent-A-Car, 142 Sheridan Street, Cairns, ph (070) 315 500.
National Inter Rent, 143 Abbott Street, Cairns, ph (070) 514 600.
Cairns 4WD Hire, 55 Mulgrave Road, Cairns, ph (070) 510 822.

EATING OUT

Cairns has some of the best eating places in Queensland. Most of the international standard hotels and motels have at least one restaurant as well as a bistro, or the like. There is also a good selection of restaurants. Here are a few names and addresses.

Barnacle Bill's, 65 The Esplanade, ph 512 241 - licensed, seafood - open 7 nights from 5pm.

Barra's, upstairs in the Conservatory Shopping Village (Lake Street through to Abbott Street), ph 531 053 - licensed,

international a la carte cuisine - open Mon-Sat 5.30pm till late.

Ca'D'Oro, 51 Grafton Street, ph 512 198 - licensed, Italian cuisine - open Mon-Sat 6pm till late.

Cafe Seafood, 252 Sheridan Street, ph 511 122 - restaurant food at cafe prices - outdoor tables - open seven days till late.

Dundee's Bar & Grill, cnr Sheridan & Alpin Streets, ph 510 399 - licensed, seafood, steak and pasta - open 7 nights from 6pm.

Cherry Blossom, cnr Spence & Lake Streets, ph 521 050 - licensed, Japanese Sushi Bar, Tepanyaki and a la carte - open 7 nights from 6pm.

Far Horizons, Williams Esplanade, Palm Cove, ph 553 000 - licensed, beachfront seafood restaurant and bar with outdoor tables - open for breakfast, lunch and dinner.

Fox & Firkin Bar & Bistro, cnr Lake & Spence Streets, ph 315 305 - licensed, good pub meals with outdoor tables and entertainment - open Mon-Sat 11.30am-2am, Sun 4pm till late.

Greek Taverna, cnr Aplin & Grafton Streets, ph 411 500 - licensed, Greek and seafood, with outdoor tables - open Tues-Sun from 6pm till late.

Hog's Breath Cafe, 64 Spence Street, ph 317 711 - saloon and grill - open 7 days 11am-2pm, 6pm till late.

Yakanbuna, upstairs, the Conservatory Shopping Village (Lake Street through to Abbott Street), ph 314 151 - licensed, open kitchen char grill - open Tues-Fri noon-2.30pm, Tues-Sun 6pm till late.

ENTERTAINMENT

Cairns has nightclubs, discos, karaoke bars, theatre restaurants, live theatre and cinemas. There are street musicians and all types of performing artists in and around the shopping areas and taverns and bars.

Because the weather is quite warm at night there are always lots of people to be found along the Esplanade, eating at pavement tables, or picnicking on the lawns.

Cairns also has a few clubs who welcome visitors and offer free temporary membership for those who live more than 40km from the club.

Cairns Leagues Club, 139 Grafton Street, ph 311 079.

Brothers Leagues Club (Cairns), 99 Anderson Street, ph 531 053.
The Yacht Club, 4 The Esplanade (between Hilton Hotel and Great Adventures), ph 312 750.

SHOPPING

There are lots of shopping opportunities in Cairns. The large hotels have boutiques offering imported fashion items and jewellery, and then there is *The Pier Marketplace*. The Pier is a landmark in Cairns and the building contains the Radisson Plaza Hotel and the Pier Marketplace, a specialty retail leisure centre.

It has separate theme walkways, the most glamorous of which is the Governor's Way, where Cairn's best fashion stores and boutiques are found. The main entrance leads to Trader's Row, which has a colonial air and some really appealing shops that are not the usual high fashion.

The Mud Markets are held on Saturday and Sunday in the main amphitheatre of the specialty retail centre, and local artisans and artists set up stalls selling all sorts of interesting objects from handcrafts to glassware. Live entertainers roam around the markets, creating a really festive atmosphere.

The Pier Marketplace is open daily 9am-9pm, but most of the shops in the city centre are open Mon-Thurs 8.30am-8pm, Fri 8.30am-9pm, Sat 8.30am-5.30pm, Sun 3-8pm. Those in the suburbs would have shorter hours with night shopping on one night only.

SIGHTSEEING

There are no sandy beaches in Cairns itself, only mudflats, but prolific birdlife gathers there. Palms line many streets, with parks and gardens displaying a riot of colour from bougainvillea, hibiscus, poinciana and other tropical blooms. The old part of town is to be found around Wharf Street and The Esplanade. The National Trust has put out a walking tour brochure for this part of town. *The Esplanade* is 5km long and runs along the side of the bay. This park-like area is a very pleasant place to relax in the cooler part of the day.

The Flecker Botanic Gardens, Collins Avenue, Edge Hill, are open daily and feature graded walking tracks through natural rainforest to Mount Whitfield, from where there are excellent views of the city and coastline.

Centenary Lakes, Greenslopes Street, Cairns North, are an extension of Flecker Botanic Gardens and were created to mark the city's centenary in 1976. There are two lakes, one fresh water the other salt, and bird life abounds. Mount Mooroobool (610m) in the background is the city's highest peak. There are barbecue facilities in the reserve.

The Pier Marketplace hosts live entertainment daily, and is the departure point for most reef cruises and fishing boat charters. Sit on the verandah and enjoy a snack or meal from one of the many food outlets, while taking in the magnificent views over Trinity Inlet. The Jabiru Dance Troupe perform Aboriginal and Islander dances here every evening.

The paddlewheeler, SS *Louisa*, departs from the Marlin Jetty, Trinity Inlet, daily at 10am and 3pm for a still-water cruise.

The *Royal Flying Doctor Service*, 1 Junction Street, Edge Hill, ph 535 687, is open daily 8.30am-5pm. It has audio-visual displays that outline the operations of the "radio-medical" service and the "school of the air". There is a small admission fee.

Sugarworld Gardens, Mill Road, Edmonton, ph 555 477, is 14km south of Cairns, and has tropical horticulture, a licensed restaurant, sugarmill tours, camel rides and waterslides. The complex is open daily 9am-5pm.

INLAND FROM CAIRNS

The fertile Mareeba, Atherton and Evelyn Tablelands rise in three gigantic steps from the coastal plains. Jungle fringed volcanic crater lakes, waterfalls and fertile farmlands, coupled with the only temperate climate in the Australian tropics, lure many visitors to the Tablelands each year. Views from the lookouts on the Kuranda, Gillies, Rex and Palmerston Highways are spectacular.

Kuranda, a tiny mountain hamlet in the rainforest, is the first stop-off on the Tableland journey. The town can be reached by train from Cairns and the ride passes waterfalls and stunning views to the coast before ending at a picturesque station. Kuranda has many attractions: Australia's only permanent Aboriginal theatre presents daily shows based on Dreamtime legends; the largest butterfly farm in the world, listed in the Guinness Book of Records; a noctarium that provides a close-up look at the rarely seen nocturnal inhabitants of the rainforests; cruises on the Barron River; and guided walks into the jungle. The town's main street is lined with galleries, shops and restaurants, and the terraced markets are the biggest and best in the north. While in Kuranda you may be tempted to try bungy jumping, then again you might prefer to watch other "brave" people trying it.

For more information on Kuranda here are a few telephone numbers: the train journey, ph (070) 526 249; Tjapukai Dance Theatre, ph (070) 937 544; Frogs Restaurant, ph (070) 937 405; Kuranda Noctarium, ph (070) 937 334; Trading Post Restaurant, ph (070) 937 166; Kuranda Rainforest Tours, ph (070) 937 476; Kuranda Markets, ph (070) 938 772; Butterfly Sanctuary, ph (070) 937 575; Kuranda Orchids, ph (070) 938 767.

The **Mareeba/Dimbulah** district, approximately 66km west of Cairns, is the largest tobacco growing area in Australia.

Atherton, with its red volcanic soil, is the central town of the Atherton Tablelands. Maize silos dominate the skyline.

Malanda is in the heart of tropical Australia's only viable dairying district. The Malanda milk factory boasts the longest milk run in the world that extends as far as Darwin in the Northern Territory.

Millaa Millaa is the waterfall capital of the Tablelands, taking in the Millaa Millaa, Zillie and Elinjaa Falls.

Millstream Falls, south of Ravenshoe, when in flood are the widest waterfalls in Australia.

Herberton is the north's historic mining town, and tin is still produced in the area.

Irinebank, situated near Herberton, is steeped in history. Its tin crushing plant has been in operation since 1890, and it has other historic buildings.

Ravenshoe is situated on the western side of the Evelyn Tablelands, and is the gateway to the back country and gemfields of the north. It is a major timber town providing some of Australia's most beautiful woods. Close by is Koombooloomba Dam and Tully Falls, with many walking tracks to Eyrie Lookout.

Some of the individual Tableland attractions include Tinaroo Dam, the Crater National Park, the twin crater lakes of Eacham and Barrine, and the Curtin Fig Tree. Further north of the Evelyn Tablelands is the Chillagoe Caves National Park which is accessible by road and air charter from Cairns.

DIVING

The following companies in Cairns offer diving trips/lessons.

Pro Dive, Marlin Parade, ph (070) 315 255 - 5 day learn to dive courses are held 4 times weekly. 3 day/2 night liveaboard cruises 4 times weekly - PADI 5-Star facility.

Blue Horizon Divers 133 Abbot Street, ph (070) 313 805 - daily trips to the Outer Barrier Reef on board the *Horizon Seeker* - certified divers, introductory dives, snorkelling, 5-star PADI Centre, retail store.

Deep Sea Divers Den, The Pier Marketplace, 319 Draper Street, ph (070) 315 622/3 - dive and snorkel trips, dive courses (beginner to instructor level), diving/fishing charters on the Outer Barrier Reef.

Taka Dive, PO Box 6592, ph (070) 518 722 - offer dives in Cod Hole, Ribbon Reefs, Coral Sea - liveaboard, departs bi-weekly.

Great Diving Adventures Cairns, ph (070) 510 455 - PADI open water dive courses available on tropical Fitzroy Island, including accommodation, meals, transfers and certification - other great dive locations include Norman Reef and Michaelmas Cay, both on the Outer Barrier Reef.

CAIRNS

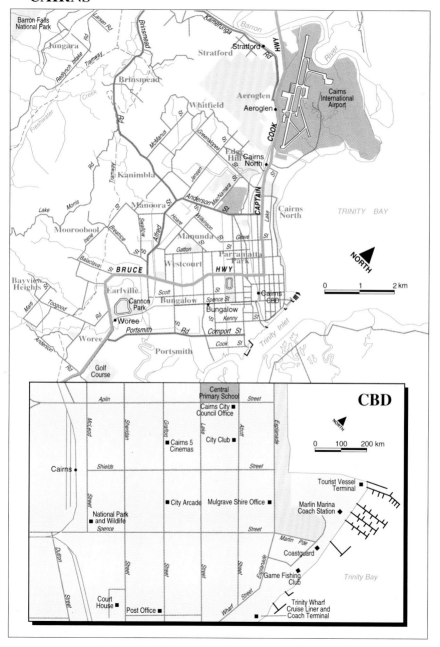

CAIRNS to COOKTOWN

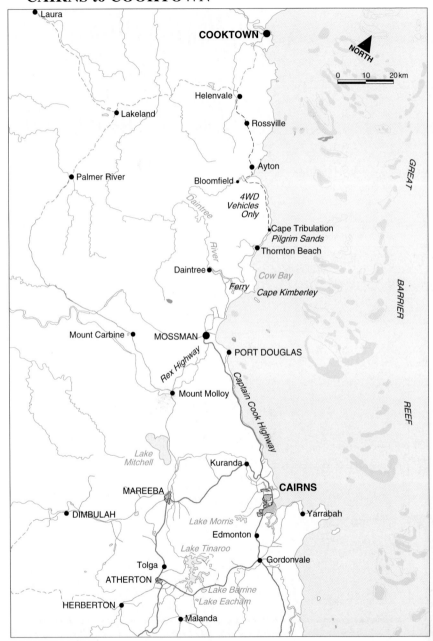

TOURS

The *Cairns Explorer* bus leaves from Lake Street Transit Mall every hour 9am-4pm Mon-Sat. It visits Wescourt shopping, Earlville shopping, Freshwater swimming hole, Freshwater Connection, Mangrove Boardwalk, Botanical Gardens, Flying Doctor, Centenary Lakes. For bookings and enquiries, ph (070) 551 240.

Wait A-While Rainforest Tours, PO Box 6647, Cairns, 4870, ph (070) 331 153 - day/night wildlife tours - the best way to see the rainforest, birds and animals of North Queensland - small groups, 4WD, experienced guides - departs 2pm daily.

Cairns Scenic Day Tours, 198-200 McCormack Street, ph (070) 321 381, specialise in Kuranda Scenic Railway, Atherton Tablelands, Port Douglas and Daintree "Crocodile Country Tours".

Tropic Wings Luxury Coach Tours (Gray Line, ph (070) 353 555, specialise in day tours around Cairns and The Tropical North - Atherton Tablelands, Port Douglas & Daintree, Cape Tribulation, Chillagoe, 3 day Outback and Gulf.

Down Under Tours, PO Box 5570, Cairns, 4871, ph (070) 331 355, offer tours to Kuranda, Daintree/Port Douglas, The Tablelands, Cairns and Orchid Valley, Weatherby Station (outback).

Australian Pacific Tours, 107 Draper Street, Cairns - 24 hour reservations (070) 519 299 7am-8pm, 313 371 8pm-7am - they have an extensive range of half and full days tours, as well as extended tours from 2 to 12 days.

Wilderness Challenge, PO Box 254, Cairns,4870, ph (070) 556 504 - 4WD adventure safaris from 1 to 14 days or charters - travel to Cape York, Hinchinbrook, Cooktown, Daintree, Kakadu, Lava Tubes, etc.

Billy Tea Bush Safaris, PO Box 77 North Cairns, 4870, ph (070) 537 115 - 1 day to 14 day safaris available to Cape York, Alice Springs, Ayers Rock, etc.

Oz Tours Safaris, PO Box 6464, Cairns, 4870, ph toll free within Australia (008) 079 006 - 7, 9, 10 and 12 day overland/air or 16 day all overland Cape York safaris. Both camping or accommodated options available - also Cairns-Cape York-Thursday Island.

CRUISES

Reef-Jet Cruises, The Pier Marketplace, ph (070) 315 559 - Green Island Half Day Cruises - depart Cairns 8.45am arrive Cairns 12.30pm - depart Cairns 1pm arrive Cairns 5pm - the full day version leaves Cairns 8.45am and returns 5pm.

Sunlover Cruises, Trinity Wharf, (PO Box 835) Cairns, ph (070) 311 055 - luxurious travel aboard Super-Cats to Moore or Arlington Reef - most innovative reef pontoons afloat, underwater theatre and marine touch tanks, free guided snorkelling tours, delicious buffet lunch - free semi-sub (Moore Reef), Supa Viewer (Arlington Reef), and glass bottom boat rides - all levels of diving catered for - optional helicopter and sea plane joyflights (Moore Reef only) - free guided rainforest walk on Fitzroy Island.

Ocean Spirit Cruises, PO Box 2140, Cairns, 4870, ph (070) 312 920 - daily departures aboard either sailing vessel *Ocean Spirit I* or *Ocean Spirit II* to either Michaelmas or Upolu Cay - delicious tropical seafood buffet available.

Big Cat, The Pier Marketplace, ph (070) 518 896, has cruises that depart daily from The Pier at 9am travel to Green Island - snorkelling, glass bottom boat tours, lunch served on board, submersible reef coral viewer, guided snorkel tours - return Cairns 5pm.

Captain Cook Cruises, Trinity Wharf, ph (070) 314 433, offer 3, 4 and 7 day Reef

Escape cruises every week - cruise to Hinchinbrook and Dunk Islands, or Cooktown and Lizard Island.

Coral Princess Barrier Reef and Island Cruises, cnr Aplin & Sheridan Streets, ph (070) 311 041 - sails between Cairns and Townsville called at island resorts and uninhabited islands for beachcombing, swimming and a tropical barbecue.

Clipper Sailaway Cruises, PO Box 2377, Cairns, 4870, ph (070) 312 516 - sail on SV *Atlantic Clipper*, Australia's largest passenger sailing ship - 140' sailing ship catering for 34 passengers - cruises from Cairns to Lizard Island, Great Barrier Reef, Cape York.

SCENIC FLIGHTS

Tiger Moth Scenic Flights & Joy Rides - their ads read, "The scenery, the music of the wind in the wires, the sheer exhilaration and freedom! It's the only way to fly." If this sounds good to you, contact Hangar 8, Cairns Airport, ph (070) 561 530 (after hours) or mobile 018 770 669.

Peninsula Mail Runs by Cape York Air Services, ph (070) 359 399, have 7 scheduled runs per week to over 100 stations, dropping in some of the world's most remote cattle stations.

FITZROY ISLAND

Fitzroy has an area of 4 sq km, and is situated 26km south-east of Cairns. It is only 6km from the mainland and was named by Captain Cook after the Duke of Grafton, a politician of the time.

The island has only had a resort since 1981, and it is currently operated by Great Adventures, who also operate the resort on Green Island.

In 1819 Phillip King reported that Welcome Bay, where the resort is, was a good anchorage for passing ships because of its fresh water and supplies of timber.

In 1877 Fitzroy was made a place of quarantine where Chinese immigrants were to stay for 16 days before completing their journey to the Queensland gold fields. At one stage there were 3000 of them in residence, which lead to near-riot conditions, and is the reason for the Chinese graves that are to be found, not the Smallpox that the authorities feared.

Fitzroy Island is not a great place for swimming as the beaches tend to be corally rather than sandy, although Nudey Beach has some sand. There are a few walking trails - the round trip to the lighthouse; a short rainforest walk to the Secret Garden; and the walk to Nudey Beach.

HOW TO GET THERE

Great Adventures has a fast catamaran service that leaves Cairns daily at 8.30am and 10.30am daily, and leaves Fitzroy at 4.30pm daily. Fares are $23 adult return, $11.50 child return, $57.50 family return.

ACCOMMODATION

The **Resort** has villas and beach houses.

Record facilities are: restaurant, bar, kiosk, dive shop, laundry/ironing facilities, swimming pool, boutique, EFTPOS.

Villa facilities are: private facilities, colour TV, hairdryer, tea/coffee making facilities, iron/board, refrigerator, ceiling fans, room serviced daily.

Beach house facilities are: shared rooms, shared bathrooms, linen and blankets, shared kitchen facilities, fans.

Tariffs for one night per person is:

Beach House Share (room only) 1-4 people - $26

Beach House Private (room only) 2 people - $44

Villa (includes dinner & breakfast) 2 people - $156.

Children's tariffs are: 0-3 years - free

4-14 years - Villa (D&B) - $73

Beach House - adult rates.

The rate for the villas also includes use of beach equipment.

Reservations can be made through Great Adventures in Cairns, ph (070) 515 644, or direct through the resort, Fitzroy

Island, PO Box 2120 Cairns, 4870, ph (070) 519 588, fax (070) 521 335.

There is a camping ground on the island that is owned by the local shire council, but managed by Great Adventures, so permits to stay there must be obtain from their office on Wharf Street in Cairns. Daily rates are around $10, and there are barbecues and cold showers.

The Rainforest Restaurant at the resort is open to people staying in the beach houses or camping, but it is not a cheap night out.

There is a mini-market near the beach house bungalows that has a range of supplies for those who want to cook for themselves.

DIVING

There is good diving water right off-shore, and the Reef is not far away. The resort dive shop hires out all gear for snorkelling and diving, runs courses, and daily trips to Moore Reef.

GREEN ISLAND

The island has an area of 13ha and is 27km south east of Cairns. It is a true coral cay surrounded by coral reefs, and has the only 5-star resort on a coral cay in Great Barrier Reef Marine Park.

The island grew out of debris washed from its surrounding platform of coral, and is gradually being pushed north-west by prevailing currents. The waters abound with sea life, and the beach is quite beautiful. It only takes about 20 minutes to walk around the island, passing tropical vegetation, fringing casuarinas and pandanus.

Green Island's Underwater Observatory is a well known attraction. From 5m below the surface, the ever-changing panorama of marine life can be seen through portholes. Marineland Melanesia has been the island's main attraction for many years. If features two of the largest salt water crocodiles in captivity, Oscar and Cassius, as well a museum, gallery, aquarium, and large tanks with turtles and stingrays. It has interesting displays of Melanesian tribal art, and a collection of early Coral Sea sailing relics.

Incidentally, the island was also named by Captain Cook, after his chief astronomer.

Green Island is very popular with day trippers.

HOW TO GET THERE

Great Adventures has a daily fast catamaran service that departs Cairns at 8.30am, 10.30am, 3.30pm. It leaves Green Island at 9.30am, 2.30pm and 4.30pm, and these transfers are included in the tariff if staying at the resort.

ACCOMMODATION

The **Resort** has deluxe guest rooms and reef suites.

Resort facilities are: restaurants, pool bar, 2 swimming pools, resort shops, dive centre, sailboards, snorkelling, surf skis, canoes, nature activities, guest reception lounge in Cairns.

Unit facilities are: private bathroom with shower and bath, tea/coffee making facilities, air conditioning, ceiling fans, mini bar, refrigerator, colour TV, inhouse movies, IDD/STD telephone, balcony, in-room safe, bath robes.

Tariffs for one night per person/twin share are:

Deluxe rooms - $383 adult, $209 child 4-14

Reef Suite - $432 adult, $234 child 4-14.

The above rates are for full board and include free use of beach hire equipment, guest library, underwater observatory, snorkelling equipment, fish feeding and activities, and transfers ex Cairns.

Reservations can be made through your travel agent, Great Adventures in Cairns, ph (070) 515 644, or through the Resort direct, Green Island Resort, PO Box 898, Cairns, 4870, ph (070) 514 644, fax (070) 521 511.

CAPTAIN COOK HIGHWAY

THE MARLIN COAST

The Marlin Coast area extends from Machans Beach, at the mouth of the Barron River 13km north of Cairns, to Ellis Beach passing by Holloways Beach, Yorkeys Knob, Clifton Beach, Palm Cove and Kewarra Beach.

Trinity Beach and Clifton Beach are popular holiday destinations, and Palm Cove and Kewarra Beach have international resorts.

All beaches have picnic areas and regular bus services to and from Cairns. Watersporters can hire catamarans, windsurfers and surf skis at most of the major beaches in the area.

Other attractions on the highway in this area are: Paradise Palms Golf Course at Clifton Beach, ph (070) 591 166; Wildworld, a tropical parkland about 22km north of Cairns that is open daily, ph (070) 553 669 Hartley's Creek Crocodile Farm, ph (070) 553 576, open daily 9am-5pm with the main show at 3pm;

PORT DOUGLAS

Port Douglas is 75km north of Cairns, and the drive covers some of the most spectacular coastal belt and beaches in Australia. The Captain Cook Highway is wedged between towering forest-covered mountains and the Coral Sea.

Situated 6km east of the highway, Port Douglas is one of the closest towns to the Great Barrier Reef. It has the charm of a fishing port tastefully combined with modern tourism facilities.

It was settled in 1877 as the main port for the Palmer River goldfields, and today it is a popular departure point for

Cape Tribulation

professional and amateur fishermen, for trips to the outer Reef and islands, and for scuba diving and aquatic sports. The township is accessible by road, air (helicopter) and by sea.

A number of tours may be taken from the town, including horsetrail riding, a regular catamaran service to Cooktown, rainforest hiking, 4WD safaris, coach and Reef tours.

ACCOMMODATION

Following is a selection with prices for a double room per night, which should be used as a guide only. The telephone area code is 070.

Sheraton Mirage Port Douglas, Port Douglas Road, ph 995 888 - 297 hotel units, 98 two, three & four bedroom villa units - licensed restaurants, bars, swimming pool, spa, sauna, gymnasium, playground, tennis golf - hotel units $400-580; villa units $650-950 - tariff includes use of a resort facilities and transfer from Cairns Airport.

Radisson Royal Palms Resort, Port Douglas Road, ph 995 577 - 301 units - licensed restaurant, bistro, swimming pool, pool bar, spa, gymnasium, playground, tennis, putting green, volleyball, jogging tracks, kid's club, courtesy transfers from Cairns airport - $155.

Rusty Pelican Motor Inn, 123 Davidson Street, ph 995 266 - licensed restaurant (Tues-Sun), cocktail bar, swimming pool, barbecue facilities - $79-95.

Lazy Lizard Motor Inn, 121 Davidson Street, ph 995 900 - 22 units, swimming pool, spa, playground - $75-90.

Port Douglas Motel, 9 Davidson Street, ph 995 248 - 19 units, swimming pool - $62-74.

Caravan Parks

Glengarry Caravan Park, Mowbray River Road, ph 985 922 - kiosk, bbq facilities, recreation room, swimming pool, boat parking - powered sites $14; tent sites $12; cabins $45.

Four Mile Beach Caravan Park, off Barrier Street, beachfront, ph 985 281 - shop, bbq facilities - powered sites $14; tent sites $13; unit $50; on-site van $35.

Kulau Caravan Park, 24 Davidson Street, ph 995 449 - swimming pool, camp kitchen, bbq facilities - powered sites $14; tent sites $13; cabin $45.

Pandanus Van Park & Guest House, Davidson Street, ph 995 944 - shop, bbq facilities, swimming pool - powered sites $14; tent sites $12; cabin $42-57.

SIGHTSEEING

Flagstaff Hill offers a great view out over Four Mile Beach. The **Rainforest Habitat**, ph (070) 993 235, has over 300m of elevated walkway with thousands of butterflies, native birds, crocodiles, koalas and wallabies set amongst waterways and shaded tropical gardens. It is open daily and is worth seeing. The complex has won Tourism Awards.

Near the Marina Mirage is **Ben Cropp's Shipwreck Museum**, with nautical exhibits of historical significance. Open daily.

Wetherby Outback Experience is a tour to a huge working cattle station, ph (070) 995 051 for more details.

Bloomfield Track 4WD Safaris, Macrossan Street, Port Douglas, ph (070) 995 665, offer holiday packages to Daintree and Cape Tribulation national parks, and Cooktown.

Mossman is only 20km north of Port Douglas in the heart of the Mossman Valley. It is a sugar town surrounded by green mountains, the highest being Mt Demi at 1158m.

As the business centre of the Douglas Shire, Mossman has wide tree-lined streets, colourful gardens and a large sugar mill. Guided tours of the mill are conducted during the cane crushing season (June to December), ph (070) 981 400.

The **Bally Hooley Steam Express** travels through Mossman and its countryside to the sugar mill.

A few minutes drive from the township, in a sealed road, is the Mossman Gorge in **Daintree National Park** (56,500ha). The gorge has a series of waterfalls, picnic ground, swimming facilities, and walking tracks through spectacular tropical rainforest.

The township of **Daintree** nestles in the heart of the Daintree River catchment basin, 36km north of Mossman, and entirely surrounded by the rainforest clad McDowall Ranges.

The area has an abundance of native plant-life, birds, exotic tropical butterflies and Australia's pre-historic reptile, the estuarine crocodile, can be seen in the mangrove-lined creeks and tributaries of the Daintree River.

A **Daintree River "Train"** leaves from the Cape Tribulation Ferry Crossing daily at 10.30am and 1.30pm. For those with their own transport, a vehicular ferry operates daily from 6am as crossing the river is the only way to gain access to Cape Tribulation National Park.

The 17,000ha National Park is a wilderness region north of the Daintree River. It has some of the best undeveloped coastal scenery and rainforest in Queensland. It should be noted that caution must be exercised if driving a conventional vehicle, even one with high clearance, and during and after rain a 4WD vehicle is essential. The 32km narrow, unsealed Cape Tribulation/Bloomfield Road is recommended for 4WD only, and towing caravans should not be attempted. The famous "bouncing stones" are just north of Thornton's Beach.

Cooktown is 330km north of Cairns on the banks of the Endeavour River. It sits were Captain Cook beached the *Endeavour* after she had been holed on a coral reef. Every June the town stages a re-enactment of Cook's landing as part of the Cooktown Discovery Festival.

Relics of Cook's visit and the town's early history are housed in the **James Cook Museum** in the Sir Joseph Banks Gardens.

Cooktown Sea Museum and Tourist Information Centre in Walker street has an extensive collection of marine exhibits. They can also advise on 4WD and air safari type adventures to the Quinkan Aboriginal Art Galleries near Laura, to Lizard Island, and north to the tip of Cape York and Thursday Island.

CRUISES

Lady Douglas, the Port Douglas paddlewheeler has four coffee cruises daily - include a ride on the Bally Hooley Train - reservations can be made at Bally Hooley Station Shop,

Marina Mirage, Port Douglas, ph (070) 995 051

Quicksilver Wavepiercer departs Marina Mirage at 10am daily and travels to Agincourt Reef, the edge of Australia's Continental Shelf - swim snorkel and view the coral from semi-submarines. Quicksilver, ph (070) 995 500.

Quicksilver Low Isles catamaran departs Marina Mirage daily at 10am for the Low Isles - swim snorkel and view coral from glass bottom boats - lunch provided.

LIZARD ISLAND

Lizard Island has an area of 21 sq km, and is the most northerly of the Barrier Reef resort islands. It is 240km from Cairns, but close to the outer Barrier Reef, and has 23 beaches that are good for swimming and snorkelling.

Captain Cook and Dr Joseph Banks landed on Lizard Island, after they had repaired the *Endeavour* at what is now Cooktown. They named it after the many large lizards they found there.

Shell middens found around the island testify to the fact that Aborigines had made it their home, and it is thought that parts of the island had some sacred meaning for them. This is given as the possible reason for a tragedy that occurred in the early 1880s. Robert and Mary Watson lived on the island and collected beche-de-mer (sea slugs), a Chinese delicacy. Robert left Mary and her baby with two Chinese servants for company while he went off in search of new fishing grounds. Whilst he was away some Aborigines arrived on the island and killed one servant and wounded the other. Mary decided to leave the island, so she loaded the baby and the remaining servant into an iron tank and set off for the mainland. They never made it, and their bodies were discovered some months later on one of the Howick islands.

It is thought that inadvertently the Watsons may have interfered with an Aboriginal sacred site, thus causing the attack. The ruins of the Watson's house can still be seen, near the top of Cook's Look.

Lizard has over 1000ha of National Park, and some good walks. The climb to the top of Cook's Look is the most popular, and is well signposted, and from the Resort it is a short walk to the ruins of the Watson house. The waters around the island are home to coral reefs and countless tropical fish, including the renowned Black Marlin. From August to November it attracts fishermen worldwide.

HOW TO GET THERE

By air from Cairns by *Sunstate Airlines*. The flight takes about one hour. There are no regular ferry or boat services to Lizard Island, but it is included as a destination in some of the cruises run by Captain Cook Cruises, ph (070) 314 433.

ACCOMMODATION

The **Resort** comprises 30 standard suites and two deluxe suites, the Marlin Centre and the Lodge, with a small shop, the club-like lounge and bar with a recorded history of the island's biggest catches, and the restaurant. The restaurant, bar and rooms have recently been refurbished.

Resort facilities are: restaurant, lounge and bar, swimming pool, tennis courts, laundry service, boutique, paddle skis, outboard dinghies, catamarans, sailboarding, snorkelling, Outer Barrier Reef trips, Eco tours, basic fishing gear, glass-bottom boat trips, scuba diving/resort training, waterskiing, boat and game fishing charters, EFTPOS.

Suite facilities are: private bathroom, refrigerator, mini-bar, air-conditioning, IDD/STD telephone, ironing facilities, daily cleaning service, writing desk, private verandah, and the deluxe suites have separate living area.

Tariffs for one night per person/twin share are: Executive - $430 adult, $215 child 6-14; Deluxe - $490 adult, $245 child 6-14.
The above rates include all meals and free use of snorkelling gear, water skiing, tennis, surf skis, windsurfers, catamarans, basic fishing gear and outboard dinghies.
Not included in the rates are game fishing boats and dive facilities. Note that children under 6 years of age are not

welcome. Reservations can be made through your travel agent, any Qantas office, or the resort itself, Private Mail Bag 40, Cairns, Qld, 4870, ph (070) 603 999, fax (070) 603 991.
Credit cards accepted: Visa, MasterCard, Bankcard, Diners Club, American Express, JCB.

Camping

There is a camping area at Watson's Bay, with the following facilities - toilets, drinking water, picnic tables, barbecues. Rates are $5/site/night ($30/site/week) for up to six people, and for further information and reservations contact QNP&WS, PO Box 2066 Cairns, 4870, (070) 523 096.

DIVING

Some consider that Lizard Island has the best diving along the Great Barrier Reef, and in fact is surrounded by excellent reefs. **The Ribbon Reefs** lie only a 20 minute boat ride from the island. These are comprised of a string of ten coral ramparts that support an immense undersea world of living coral and sea animals, and the most spectacular underwater scenery. All the Ribbon Reefs are great, but following are some highlights.

The Code Hole is world renowned and very popular. It is at the northern tip of Reef No. 10, and divers can hand feed giant Potato Cod, some over 2.5m in length.

Pixie Pinnacle is a coral bommie on the southern end of Reef No. 10. Here divers will find species of pelagic fish, black coral, and a host of tropical fish.

Dynamite Pass is a narrow area of water just north of Ribbon Reef No. 10. the depths range is from 4m to 40m below the surface, but visibility is about 30m and there is plenty to see.

Detached Reefs are located in the Coral Sea half-way between Cooktown and Cape York. Both reefs extend from a metre or so under the surface to the seabed some 500m below. This is sheer wall diving at its best with visibility extending more than 40m. Expect to see giant sponges, sea whips, Angelfish, Clownfish, Manta Rays, shark & varieties of coral.

INDEX